Praise for *Anti-Time Management*

"Heart-touching and awe-inspiring! Richie Norton has faced too many hardships for one lifetime. But he's come out the other side with a life-embracing framework to help you reclaim your time—and live your dreams."

—**Susan Cain,** #1 *New York Times* Bestselling Author of *Bittersweet* and *Quiet*

"We all look at time totally wrong! Richie Norton will totally reshape how you use, not abuse your time. We think lack of time is our problem when it's really lack of attention. If you want to stop having time own you, gain total control, free yourself to do what's really important, make time start working for you, gain the power to prosper, master true performance power . . . oh, and actually 'game change' your brain ALL in one or two can't-put-down reads—this book is the key!"

—**Jay Abraham,** America's #1 Marketing Expert

"Richie's words rewired my brain and touched my heart. His techniques immediately shifted my perspective and made my future accessible in the now. His insights and questions made me restructure the way I prioritize my mind and therefore my life."

—**Sirah,** Grammy Award–Winning Artist

"Powerful! *Anti-Time Management* will help you clarify and prioritize what is really important for your life, and for your time. Richie Norton's writing is moving and profound with personal stories that will keep you engaged cover to cover."

—**Dr. Marshall Goldsmith,** Thinkers50 #1 Executive Coach and *New York Times* Bestselling Author of *Triggers, Mojo,* and *What Got You Here Won't Get You There*

"Potent . . . poignant . . . practical . . . inspiring . . . wise. If you want to put your dreams at the front of your timeline, Richie Norton will teach you how. A brilliant successor to *The 4-Hour Workweek.* Bravo!"

—**Whitney Johnson,** CEO of Disruption Advisors, a Top Ten Business Thinker as Named by Thinkers50

"Richie Norton is absolutely brilliant—and he's done it again! This is an amazing book that is filled with breakthrough insights while simultaneously being immensely practical and immediately useful. Richie simplifies complex layers of work-life freedom that we all grapple with such that I'm already creating more space for my life, family and business in ways that inspire me, give me hope, and bring me joy—and I'm confident he can do the same for you!"

—**Stephen M. R. Covey,** *New York Times* and #1 *Wall Street Journal* Bestselling Author of *The Speed of Trust* and *Trust & Inspire*

"Richie Norton always brings a killer combination of strategy, values, and heart to anything he does. *Anti-Time Management* is no exception. It has the perfect combination of pragmatic frameworks and revolution-invoking motivation. If you read this book and follow its advice, you will come out a clearer, happier, and more productive person."

—**Pamela Slim,** Author of *Escape from Cubicle Nation* and *The Widest Net*

"*Anti-Time Management* brings the fire! This book will unleash your ability to transform your time into freedom in ways you've never dreamed. Richie and I have worked together for years using the *Time Tipping* principles he teaches to make complex projects profitable. Richie Norton will show you how to automate what you don't want to do to support your autonomy in everything you do want to do. You'll find joy in becoming a *Time Tipper*, as I have."

—**John Lee Dumas,** Bestselling Author of *The Common Path to Uncommon Success*, Award-Winning Host of *Entrepreneurs on Fire*

"Richie Norton is meant to be your mentor. His latest book, *Anti-Time Management*, simplifies the essence of radically taking control of your time and thereby your life! Richie tips traditional entrepreneurial time management on its head. Instead, you'll learn how to use flexibility without slipping into inconsistency. And because one size does not fit all when it comes to goal setting—you'll love his uniquely flexible approach. Save yourself from burnout . . . Read this book!"

—**Chalene Johnson,** Lifestyle and Business Expert, Speaker, *New York Times* Bestselling Author, and Top-Ranked Podcaster

"If you're looking to start something new, you need time, and if you want the blueprint for how to actually get things done, *Anti-Time Management* is it. Richie has broken down the exact ways you need to take control of your time and manage in a way that gives you results. I've worked with Richie and have used a lot of these strategies myself, and I can 100 percent vouch for what this book will do to change your life."

—**Pat Flynn,** CEO of Flynndustries and Host of the *Smart Passive Income Podcast*

"Richie Norton has written a book about freedom that will change the way we think about time management forever. You'll learn how to think long-term and take the right steps to create the life you want."

—**Dorie Clark,** *Wall Street Journal* Bestselling Author of *The Long Game* and Executive Education Faculty, Duke University Fuqua School of Business

"Richie Norton's *Anti-Time Management* follows a pattern that's helped me become one of the most streamed recording artists of our time . . . and I do piano music. When we behold ourselves to checklists, we deny ourselves of being led by a higher power that wants us to succeed in every adventure we pursue. Thank you, Richie, for reminding me, and all of us, of our God-given power to co-create things that never were before, things that will improve the life of all those around us."

—**Paul Cardall,** No. 1 *Billboard* Artist with More than 3 Billion Streams

"In this book, Richie has served up a perfect mix of one-off lessons and life experiences combined with takeaways, action steps, and a paramount reminder that time truly is our most valuable commodity. This book is a must for anyone who wants to be prolific in what they do, without the distractions stopping them from doing it!"

—**Chris Ducker,** Bestselling Author of *Virtual Freedom: How to Work with Virtual Staff to Buy More Time, Become More Productive, and Build Your Dream Business*

"What if we decided what kind of life we wanted and then designed our work to build just that? A revolutionary concept, but one that is easier to achieve than you might think. Richie Norton shows you how he did it and how you can too. You can't walk away from reading this book without second-guessing everything."

—**Laura Gassner Otting,** *Washington Post* Bestselling Author of *Limitless: How to Ignore Everybody, Carve Your Own Path, and Live Your Best Life*

"*Anti-Time Management* absolutely blew me away. I will never think about time in the same way. Norton's message of attention prioritization and time creation is groundbreaking and will help you find harmony between work and life priorities. If you want more time in your life, you've got to read Norton's latest masterpiece."

—**Rhett Power,** Cofounder of Accountability Inc. and *Forbes* Columnist

"*Anti-Time Management* marks a new era. Read this book to prosper in life and business, and make the most of your precious time on Earth. Richie's right! Anti-time management is the new time management. Richie Norton is a longtime mentor of mine. What he teaches in this book is exactly what helped me go from broke student to seven-figure bestselling author and entrepreneur—all while enjoying my growing family without compromise. Awe-inspiring read!"

—**Dr. Benjamin Hardy,** Bestselling Author of *Be Your Future Self Now: The Science of Intentional Transformation*

"Richie is a MASTER at simplifying big ideas into actionable takeaways. Richie illuminates flaws in the way we use TIME that are impossible to unsee. This book is a step-by-step guide to designing the life you were meant for."

—**Hank Fortener,** Music Executive, Founder of AdoptTogether.org

"Being coached by Richie Norton and applying his *Time Tipping* principles is like viewing life from the summit rather than the trailhead. I went from busy lawyer with little time to joyfully living my personal values as a husband and father with time for what I love—all while my business expands to impact more lives than I ever imagined in support of our ideal lifestyle. *Anti-Time Management* is productivity unhinged. This will have a generational impact on my family. It is legacy-building in the most important facets of life. You cannot put a price on the value to business, life, and family that Richie delivers."

—**AJ Green,** CEO of Grnobl Land Co.

ANTI-TIME MANAGEMENT

Reclaim Your Time and Revolutionize Your Results with the Power of Time Tipping

RICHIE NORTON

Go
hachette
BOOKS
New York

Hachette Go, an imprint of Hachette Books
Hachette Book Group
1290 Avenue of the Americas
New York, NY 10104
HachetteGo.com
Facebook.com/HachetteGo
Instagram.com/HachetteGo

First Paperback Edition: August 2023

Hachette Books is a division of Hachette Book Group, Inc.

Print book interior design by Jeff Williams

Library of Congress Control Number: 2022937650

ISBNs: 9780306827068 (hardcover); 9780306827075 (trade paperback); 9780306827082 (ebook)

Printed in the United States of America

LSC-C

Printing 1, 2023

For Grif

I arise in the morning torn between a desire to improve (or save) the world and a desire to enjoy (or savor) the world. This makes it hard to plan the day.

—E. B. WHITE

Contents

ANTI-TIME MANAGEMENT: THE TIME TIPPING FRAMEWORK

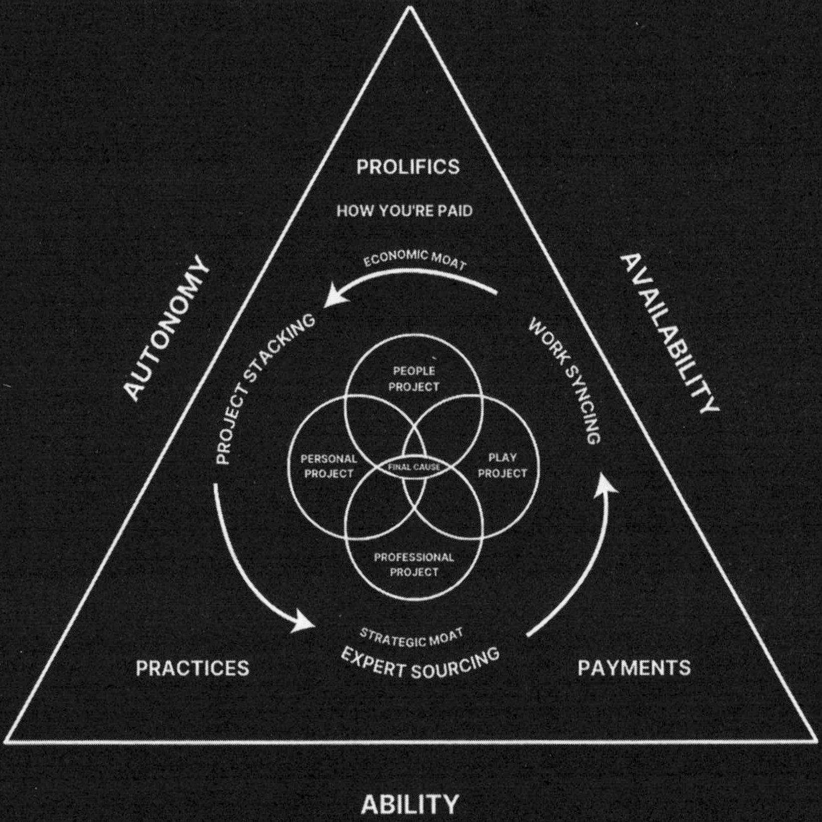

T.I.M.E.

TODAY IS MY EVERYTHING

PREFACE

TIME = Today Is My Everything

Gavin's Law: Live to Start. Start to Live.

"BALLISTIC MISSILE THREAT TO HAWAII
There is a Ballistic missile
THREAT INBOUND TO HAWAII.
Seek Immediate shelter and wait for future information."

The text message appeared on my phone while standing in a friend's living room thousands of miles away from my home and family in Hawaii.

I called my wife.

No answer.

I called my three boys.

No answer.

No answer.

No answer.

"THIS IS NOT A TEST. Reply with YES to confirm."

I called again, and my thirteen-year-old son, Cardon, answered and then stammered panicked, tearful good-byes, certain he would be dead in a matter of moments.

"I love you so much, Dad."

I sat down where I had been standing, staring off into space.

My teenage son had just said his good-byes.

I was powerless even to comfort them. Sorrow surged through my body, as this wasn't the first time I had felt powerless. Like a wheel going 'round, my world was crashing down again.

In brief flashes, my mind ricocheted from one tragedy to the next tragedy to the next tragedy to the next . . . a long list of experiences that had brought my family and me to this moment.

I remembered every step as Natalie and I walked out of the hospital, my arms wrapped around her shoulders. We'd walked into a hospital seventy-six days before for her to give birth to our fourth son, and we walked out of a different hospital with empty hearts and hands after our sweet baby boy Gavin passed away as a result of contracting whooping cough.

I remembered the day we buried Natalie's brother Gavin. It still felt like I could see our then tiny children's eyes looking at us and wondering what happened to "Unkie," who unexpectedly passed away in his sleep at age twenty-one.

I pictured our three beautiful foster children whom we lost to the system in a failed adoption and wondered how they were doing somewhere else in the world, a pain that sometimes feels worse than the death of loved ones, honestly, because there is no finality. Are they okay? Do they still know we love them?

More recent stories flooded my mind. I thought of my sweet Natalie. In the wake of that failed adoption, while on the way to the airport, she had a stroke in the car. She lost her memory. She couldn't put words together. She couldn't remember our names. She couldn't recall much of anything. I still clearly remember the terror in my heart as I tried to drive and figure out what was happening. My oldest son, Raleigh, who was twelve at the time, comforted his mom despite the fact that she couldn't say his name. I searched frantically for the nearest hospital and got off the freeway as soon as I found one.

I remember feeling scared while trying to compose myself at the hospital and their mounds of paperwork. I remember feeling almost paralyzed, hoping the situation wouldn't overcome us. We moved from one hospital to another. The doctors did all their tests and came up with, lo and behold, nothing. Nada. They recognized a stroke or ministroke had occurred but miraculously couldn't see any damage to the brain. After a couple of days, Natalie's mind and memory returned to normal with some on-and-off side effects.

The prognosis?

"It might happen again. In fact, it's likely it will happen again."

The prescription?

"Keep living your life. There is nothing you can do."

I told Natalie I thought we should skip the trip and go home as the obvious course of action. It would be better to stay in bed.

"No way," she said.

Natalie told me that if she got back in bed, she'd never get up again after having gone through so much—losing her brother, losing our baby, losing our three foster children. She wanted to show up differently for herself and our family. Considering there was no clinical prescription, why not create space for courage?

So she faced her fears and got on the plane.

As I marveled at her courage in the wake of that stroke, I knew how courageous she must be showing up in the face of this missile warning. Then my mind turned again to the next time tragedy struck.

I had been off-island on a trip as a speaker for an event and planned to go on to China to meet with new suppliers for one of my companies. It was late at night on the mainland when I received a call from a friend in Hawaii. He called twice. Then texted.

My eleven-year-old son, Lincoln, had been hit by a car.

A speeding distracted driver didn't see him crossing the road. Lincoln was so severely injured that another friend on the scene said she didn't even recognize him. I canceled my speaking gig and my trip to China and returned to Oahu immediately.

I remember arriving at yet another hospital and seeing a different son in a hospital bed. Lincoln was in a medically induced coma. He had a collapsed lung, and part of his liver was killed on impact. He suffered a lot, too many injuries to list, too many surgeries to name, including reconstructive surgery to part of his face. When he eventually came to, these were the first words that came out of his mouth:

"Can we still go shark diving?"

That's what we had planned to do for his birthday. He turned twelve in the hospital.

I remember thinking this experience might scare Lincoln from participating in life, but, like his mom, he actively creates space for courage. Every day, he's out there doing the things he wants, riding gigantic twenty-five-foot-plus waves, sailing, mountain biking, and being an all-around good kid who finds ways to serve and help others. He knows what it's like to be hurt, and he's developed a unique sense of empathy for others.

Why are these my thoughts as my family is about to be hit by a missile:

» my son's death from whooping cough

» my brother-in-law's unexpected death at twenty-one

» the loss of our three foster children after two years of uninterrupted custody

» my wife's stroke at thirty-five

» the car that hit my eleven-year-old and nearly took his life?

I reread that first warning text from the state of Hawaii, and amid the pain and fear, I thought:

"At least we lived without regret."

Our many brushes with tragedy have made us fiercely dedicated to living a *value-driven, time-centered life.* We don't wait for a future time to live our dreams. We don't wait for a kind of "maybe someday" when we *hope* to have all the money and experience those dreams might require. We live those dreams, today. We understand the brevity of life and the incomprehensible value of the currency called ***time***. We may not have it all, but we live for it all, *always.*

While people back home in Hawaii were taking cover in bathtubs and closets and prying open maintenance holes to take shelter in the sewers, I sat there helplessly safe more than four thousand miles away.

The following thirty-eight minutes were the longest of my life. We finally received the "all clear" and learned the entire fiasco was an accident—user error, more or less—not an attack by North Korea, as the government and local news stations had announced. As the adrenaline drained from my system and profound relief took its place, I couldn't help but feel gratitude and ponder the importance of that one thought—living without regret.

Gavin's Law: Live to Start. Start to Live.

When my brother-in-law Gavin passed and later my son Gavin passed, a mentor asked me what I'd learned from their short lives. I articulated what I now call Gavin's Law—*Live to Start. Start to Live.* This life motto has been shared in my works with millions of people around the world. Trauma has a funny way of changing the way you think. The loss of the two Gavins in my life forced me to reconsider how my own life was structured. And during those moments of quiet self-reflection, I considered how those words I hold dear to my heart, "Live to Start. Start to Live," had started to shape my daily life.

As those words molded me and guided my decisions, I saw how others were also starting to do the same in their own way. Family, friends, and acquaintances were transforming through their own life challenges and inner struggles. Their values were shifting, and their choices about their attention and time were also shifting.

I've been fortunate to hear from some of my readers how the principle of Gavin's Law in *The Power of Starting Something Stupid* has helped them put family, friends, and dreams first as a choice, not at the expense, of meaningful work. Money and meaning can go hand in hand.

There's an undeniable energy that comes with Gavin's Law. Living to start the ideas that press on your mind and starting to live those ideas in real life is truly the experience of a lifetime.

But It's Not About Time, It's About You

I created an acronym for the word *time* to keep my attention on high priorities and opportunities while staying with and enjoying the present:

TIME =
Today Is My Everything

I wrote this book to help you create high-trust environments with attention to time—*the mother of all resources*—for greater contribution in the service of others while leading a life of meaning and joy, despite setbacks and even tragedy.

My Intent

I hope that this message of *attention prioritization* and *time creation* shines through as a *learnable skill* that you can practice and get better at achieving.

» You'll grow personally and professionally to keep what's most important to you at the center of your life right now—*instead of making your dreams, loved ones, and big ideas wait for you to finally have time someday in an elusive, nonexistent, and distant future.*

» You'll have the fortune of making up for lost time in life, create an abundant future of happy results at work, and generate positive impact everywhere you go.

Accepting that life is insane, that bad things happen to good people, and that you can find the courage to be grateful for the good in every situation and still move forward is hard (even terrifying), but heroic.

The best inside of all of us emerges with courage.

This book can open your mind and heart to new pathways and opportunities through inventive thinking. Be brave and take a chance on yourself—even when it's not simple or easy.

Every Sunset Is an Opportunity to Reset

If you're like me, you may have more things on your mind to do than time to achieve them. I wrote this book, in part, to address that wrestle. There's something simple I do to help me appreciate each day, relieve anxiety, and make space for a new pace.

I watch the sunset.

For me, the sunset is a metaphor for the things in my life that come and go.

Ends are beginnings.

When you reset at sunset, a tragedy becomes a budding triumph, stress becomes future success, and miscommunication becomes a meaningful opportunity to build trust.

This book begins with the sunset of your aspirations and ends with the sunrise of your dreams. That means you work from who you want to be in the future (the sunset) and create paths for you to claim today (the sunrise).

Imagine the sun setting two years from now.

Reflecting, what do you hope to have become and experienced over those 730 days?

The sum of the *operationalization* of your activities between sunset to sunset makes the difference between autonomy and monotony.

What would life look like today if you had already achieved what you wanted?

What if you could create a personal ecosystem now with the essence of your ideal future that fostered, enhanced, and propelled those standards into greater degrees of reality day by day?

This book will help you discover the practice of multidimensional thinking and dynamic ways of working to live beyond traditional goal-, habit-, and strength-management hysteria.

Find the carefully, strategically, and orderly placed questions throughout this book to help you consider where you are, where you want to be, and how to *Time Tip* to get there.

Time Tipping: Beyond Time Management

Wake-up call: time management was designed as a means of wage-rate setting, not to increase the quality of your life.

More than one hundred years ago, industrialists fabricated a new adversarial relationship between humans and time with the invention of punch clocks, moving away from agrarian labor, which was informed by the sun. In his book *The Principles of Scientific Management*, first published in 1911, Frederick Winslow Taylor, who is considered the father of scientific management, wrote, "In the past the man has been first; in the future the system must be first."

"The system must be first."

Fortunately, we live at the end of an era in which time management is rooted in the principles of the Industrial Age. No longer can *big business* thrive by squeezing out every drop of blood, sweat, and tears from workers. Rather, when corporations act this way and people talk, networks are fluid and people find new work options where they can thrive. At least that's my hope of today's many options—the economy of choices.

The *value-driven, time-centered life* my family and I have created for ourselves results from choices we've made. We've created work environments for ourselves where prioritizing flexibility and attention means that *people "must be first."*

People must be first.

This *people-first* approach moves us beyond the old time-management practices aggressively marketed to exploit us and makes this a book about the now *and* creating a new future. The same way the Industrial Revolution replaced agrarian work, we now have advanced technologies, algorithms, and artificial intelligence replacing both blue- and white-collar work.

And thank goodness. *Collars come with leashes.*

Predicting the Future of Work: The Post-Management Movement

The *management revolution* happened.

"Post-management" is here.

Instead of continuing to grow larger and larger centrally, the conglomerates of our world will eventually break down into micro-enterprises and spread to stay nimble.

Leaders will be decentralized, and the leadership competency most valued will become discernment.

Managers will become entrepreneurial and more directly responsible for top-line growth and bottom-line profits.

Solopreneurs will rise because freelancers will become commodities to utilize.

Educators will have to educate differently for students preparing to thrive in rapidly shifting digital, social, political, economic, and cultural landscapes.

"Virtual reality" will be reality, and the way we work and live will become interwoven between the digital and the physical seemingly seamlessly, or meta.

"Professionals" will have to stop acting like robots and start practicing reenergized, individualized humanity at work.

Robots will do anything that a robot can possibly do.

When artificial intelligence takes over, and it will, what happens to human work?

We will collectively become more artful, thoughtful, and creative to provide value, meaning, and worthwhileness—in essence, work will become more *human*.

And at the same time, as an increasing abundance of inputs are thrown at us incessantly from every direction, we will have to develop greater skills in tuning in to what we want and tuning out what we don't. Attunement to signals, not noise, will become as much a disruptive evolution as a discerning revolution in the marketplace.

As 24/7 interconnectivity blends personal and professional time, flexible jobs and entrepreneurship will become more the norm to support and enable greater freedom, "balance," and autonomy. People will want work that provides both meaning and money as well as the ability to do it from their location of choice—or no specified location at all.

The nature of business is changing. Whatever is to come, the opportunities of today did not exist a few years ago. The same is true of your future. So we must create and enjoy what we can, while we still can, and be highly adaptable to disruption.

The principles in this book are designed to be timeless so you can navigate the opportunities and challenges as they come amid chaos and change under various circumstances. Organizing life around your priorities *versus* organizing life around whatever job comes up are two very different styles of living with decidedly different costs and returns on time. Either way, it's a choice.

> You can make your work commitments support your personal ones. Your personal life doesn't have to be sacrificed on the altar of your work.

Market forces driven by technology, global circumstance, and a taste for flexibility and autonomy have dismantled the precepts of hierarchical bureaucracy.

Welcome to the Post-Management Movement.

Work-Life Flexibility Is the Start, Not the Goal

How to work in the Post-Management Era. Work-life flexibility has become a corporate incentive. Rest assured that when a corporation provides a benefit, the benefit is for the corporation.

Has a work-life flexibility program ever left you feeling trapped in a trade-off, in a *time trap*?

A time trap looks like freedom but acts like a hamster wheel.

Often corporate flexibility "best practices" create a work culture that holds you captive at home to the job *on purpose.*

- » Have policy and procedure at work ever had a toxic grip on your life at home?
- » Is your home life at odds with the corporate stopwatch?
- » If you're stuck at your desk at home and unable to go watch your child's third-grade program, for example, how is that more flexible than being stuck at the office?
- » Does it have to be this way?

Best practices linger longer than they are welcome. Get relevant. Update and upgrade your life with continuous learning, improvement, and application.

There is an inherent risk in reprioritizing your work-life choices. The most common work-life trap is swapping one low-priority task for another low-priority task in an endless doom loop of task management versus destination creation.

Is your life doomed to endless task switching?

A calendar won't help you with that problem. Neither will the most recent time-management techniques handed down.

If you're endlessly changing one goal for another, one habit for another, or one strength for another without achieving your desired results, maybe you're not paying attention to the larger environment or the larger game being played around you.

Your level of work-life flexibility is not measured in how many hours a week you can work from home. Work-life flexibility is the fusing of three capacities: availability, ability, and autonomy.

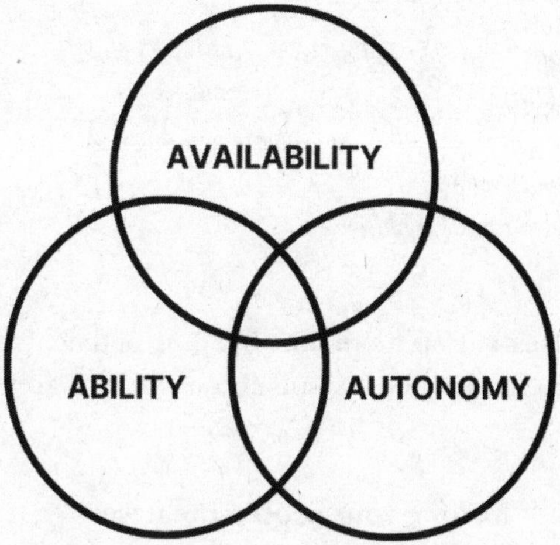

You can quickly identify your level of work-life flexibility by asking yourself how seamless it is to create the ***availability, ability,* or *autonomy*** you need to do something. For example, ask yourself these work-life flexibility questions about time, means, and choice:

» How **available** am I, *at will,* to dive deep into a new project, go on extended vacations, hang out without stress, write a book, stop working, etc., etc., etc.? Pick *anything* you've been wanting to do but haven't yet and ask yourself why.

- *What's your level of availability to make it happen?*
- *Are you free?*
- ***Do you have the time?***

» How **able** (capable) are you to do the thing you want, if you wanted to, right now?

- *What's your level of capacity and mobility to make it happen?*
- *Are you able?*
- ***Do you have the means?***

» How much **autonomy**, choice, free will, or say do you have to make this decision?

- *What's your level of decision-making to make it happen?*
- *Are you free to do as you please without negatively impacting others?*
- ***Do you have a choice?***

Work-life flexibility is more than freedom of time. Work-life flexibility is actively choosing how to spend your time for greater work-life wellness.

Making your professional work support your personal wellness is a choice.

Where *flexibility* in work and life is found in *being available, able,* and *autonomous, inflexibility* in work and life is found in being *unavailable, unable,* and *disempowered.*

The next time you say no to something you want to do at work or in life, ask yourself how flexible you're being. In what ways can you be productive without sacrificing values?

Flexibility isn't your boss's gift to give.
You must create it yourself—
even if you are your own boss.

Every choice you make can make you more available, able, and/or autonomous in one thing and/or less in another. People, places, and timing all come into play . . . and that's the point. It's one thing to be able to do something, another to be available, and another to be allowed to do it at all and vice versa.

So, how do you get true work-life flexibility? How do you experience that freeing feeling of mental work-life wellness? The key to unlocking your autonomy and having the flexibility to act on your interests is *attention prioritization.*

Good things happen not by managing time
but by prioritizing attention.

Time Tipping

Mastering your time is having the availability, ability, and autonomy to choose how you spend it and to spend it meaningfully without regret. Mastering your time goes beyond managing it. Mastering your time doesn't mean you need another planner. You don't need to create an ideal week. You don't need to try yet another productivity hack.

You don't have to work toward your dreams when you work from them. Whether you work for someone else or yourself, you can master your time.

Sometimes it may feel like everything else in your life must come before your dreams. Your "real life," as they say, can oftentimes take a backseat to your "work life." In this sense, your "real life" revolves around your work life—leaving little to no time for "real life."

Today, we have so many ways to try to "manage" our time, and know so much about it, *but we still don't have the time we need to live our real lives and pursue our dreams.*

If not time management, *then what?*

Time Tipping.

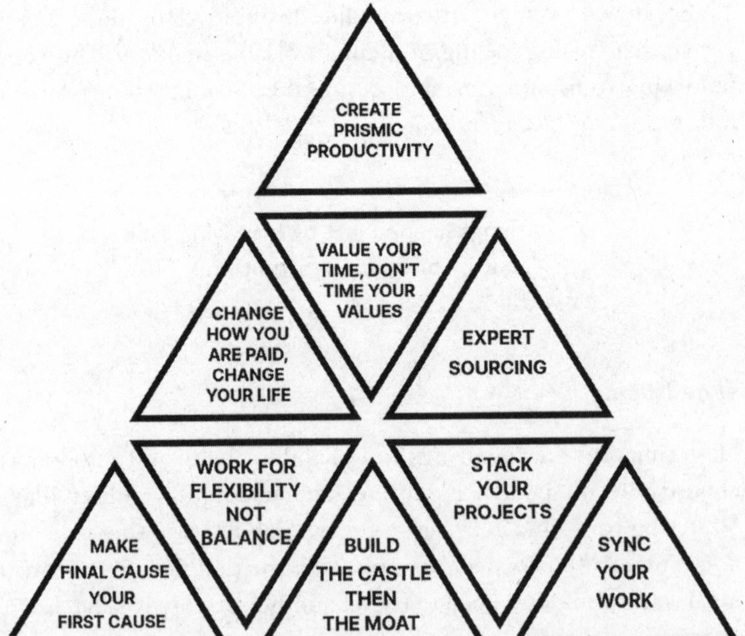

TIME = Today Is My Everything

The *Time Tipping Framework* calls for immediate application and creates a positive compound effect on your available time.

Time Tipped freedom is a strategic environment you create so that when things go wrong, you have the flexibility to fix them, prevent recurrences, and restructure for a better future.

Your ideal work style is one *Time Tipped* choice away.

Anti-Time Management will teach you how to fully embrace a time-centered, values-driven philosophy that allows achievement of life's and work's highest priorities while enjoying the freedom of time, location, and income. *Anti-Time Management* provides a strategic approach that will enable you to create more time beginning right here and right now.

To reclaim your life, start by reclaiming your time.

What Is a *Time Tipper*?

A *Time Tipper* is a person who consciously implements projects that create more time in the long term than they take in the short term.

Time Tippers begin with *Final Cause*; operate through *Project Stacking, Work Syncing,* and *Expert Sourcing*; and get paid for their *Value(s).*

Time Tipping demonstrates how two people with the same job, earning the same income, can achieve significantly different outcomes in their lives—one enjoys little or no freedom of time, while the other seems to have *all the time in the world.*

Beyond Goals, Habits, and Strengths

So, how do two people with basically the same job lead such different personal lives? They do it ***on purpose***—in three ways:

- » ***Priorities***—Good things happen by prioritizing your attention, not by managing time.
- » ***Practices***—Move from distraction to action.
- » ***Payments***—Don't turn dreams into jobs. The job of a dream is to set you free.

To tip time you'll work from your *values center* and make decisions from *Final Cause*—your *meta-goal.* Then the *Anti-Time Management Methodology* will walk you through a process to prioritize what you want to become, practice ways to free up your time for your priorities, and change how you're paid to sustain your *Time Tipped* way of life.

The *Anti-Time Management* principles show you how to make work asymmetrical by uncovering opportunities to make big results happen with small moves. I call these small moves *asymmetrical changes.*

Like a prism, you'll learn how you can focus light on one side of your life and work to create a brilliant strobe of giant life and work possibilities on the other. Implementing this methodology happens through *Project Stacking, Work Syncing,* and *Expert Sourcing.* These three principles will show you how to *expand* time by creating your own ecosystem, with structures and arrangements that streamline workflow to make more time available for the living of your aspirations, *today.*

Historically, work is locked in *where* we live and *when* we can spend our time on personal pursuits or activities, such as family, travel, and hobbies. In the past, with more traditional jobs, we had to punch a time clock and be working at specific times and specific locations. But now there is far greater flexibility about where and when you can work.

How you are paid, not necessarily how much, is the bond that binds and aligns your time—for better or worse.

Two people, for example, could be paid to produce the same exact result but have different work requirements. For instance, one person may be required to be at an office desk working from 9:00 to 5:00, while another person has the flexibility of working from their cell phone wherever they want in the world.

As an employee, changing "how" you get paid could mean renegotiating when or where or how you get results, getting a new job, or reforming how you spend your time "after hours."

The "how" of getting paid determines your quality of life. It determines the abundance of time you have to enjoy. If you have kids, *how you work* makes the difference between coaching their team, attending their recitals, putting them to bed at night . . . or not.

And honestly, what's the point of your work?

Why do you work? There is a financial incentive, fulfillment, and identity wrapped up in great work. But beyond the status quo, most people don't work for work's sake. We work for something else. What are you working for? What if you could arrange your work in such a way that it constantly supported your ability to do that *something else*?

What if, in the end, the thing you hope to do later could be done from the start?

**If you value your time,
your life will match your values.**

Time Tippers employ a strategy that allows them to prioritize their values. *Time Tippers* know that wealth is relative and what's important is planning work practices and income source(s) to fit intentions.

Sustainable *Time Tipping* means you continue to reap the benefits of your efforts repeatedly throughout your lifetime.

Create Projects to Make (Not Take) Time: The Strategic Solution

Ask yourself: If the goal is "more time," why not start with a process (or project) that creates time (not takes time)?

Creating space for more time is not an elusive, futuristic dream but something anyone can do, even engineer, from the start. I've experienced it and witnessed it. *You can too.* You can have more time as you think differently about the problems you solve and include time creation in the equation. The *Time Tipping* method shows you how to turn your attention to your priorities and put your priorities into play.

The principles of anti-time management can be applied at any level of work, collaboration, or individual project.

Here are just a few quick examples of *Time Tippers* I've worked with who changed their lives by utilizing this framework:

» A construction worker didn't want to swing a hammer anymore because his wife was sick with multiple sclerosis. They now travel the world together (as she fights MS) with their children, teaching contractors how to hire and develop tradespeople, and he now earns five times his old salary.

» A videographer, trapped in consignment work, added a new service around her values, selling related physical products—and is now making millions. She travels the world, raising her children with more time on her hands than ever.

» An executive at a growing company felt like he constantly had to step in and do the work himself—exhausting his time and health while straining his family relationships in the process. After learning how to tap into the freelancer world, he now accesses talent he didn't know existed and has expanded his company's global footprint while regaining his time, health, and personal life.

» A podcaster with a dream to invent and sell a physical product had no idea where to start. He worked with me to develop the idea, worked with my company to manufacture it, and crowdsourced funds to finance the product through presales. He is now selling products worldwide, making millions from home, while the operations and fulfillment are outsourced without consuming his time.

» A dentist with many offices and no time for the personal life of his dreams now uses virtual consults to free up his time and travels the world teaching other dentists how to get their lives back too.

» An employee shifted her in-office work priorities, thus increasing her flextime, productivity, and moneymaking opportunities without skipping a beat.

These *Time Tippers*—and many others like them—have re-created their occupation in a way that makes their everyday life feel like a special opportunity . . . because it is!

Of course, these examples are individual, but they also represent others from diverse backgrounds who have made small shifts in working to create great results in their lives. While your situation is unique, learning from those who have done it in their own sphere of influence can help you think creatively to make it work in your world. Don't discount this opportunity even if you can't see your way through it yet.

Like grief, growth is a tunnel, not a cave.

And in today's global, interconnected world, there's perhaps never been a better opportunity to strategically organize your life and work on your own terms.

Time Tippers create enormous value and free up tons of time so they can dedicate their lives to many things or dedicate more time to the things they want most in life.

Own Your Time, Own Your Life

Money isn't something you have to wait for to reclaim your time and choice. Natalie and I collected and recycled cans to make ends meet in our first years of marriage. We chose to forgo couches for a season because the thought of a couch over our next airplane ticket hurt our heads more than our butts on the floor.

Whether I was taking jobs washing dishes or taking out the trash as a part-time custodian at night while Natalie was taking on photo shoots to support our family, we've done our best to keep what's most important to us at the center of our lives regardless of income.

I'm an entrepreneur, and because of my life's experience, my life's work has revolved around creating businesses and helping other entrepreneurs create businesses that return dividends in time availability as well as money. I've had the privilege of working with Fortune 500 companies in achieving "stupid" results using *Time Tipping*, creativity, and change to help humanize the systems with personalization for greater productivity and flourishing. I've built companies to streamline processes so that people can get their natural autonomy back and live life with extra room to grow.

Regardless of the product or service, my work revolving around generating autonomy, creating freedom of time, and helping others do the same led me to write this book. You should see the look on a stranger's face when I try to explain how building tiny homes or mass-producing yoga pants are one and the same to me. When creating disposable time is the objective without sacrificing on the financials, work is simply performed differently.

For example, the freedom that *Time Tipping* has provided our family has helped us live our values better. We've done "road school" coast-to-coast for six months from New York to San Diego and border-to-border from Mexico to Canada without planning where we'd stay at night or for how long. We've traveled Europe for months at a time. It wouldn't be a surprise to find us on a humanitarian trip in Nicaragua, singing karaoke in Osaka, hanging clothes to dry outside a colorful casa in Cinque Terre, exploring the Great Wall of China, fishing in Santorini, or searching for Harry Potter locations in Scotland. Our "vacations" can last several months at a time—if we want.

The money we used for these trips was made on the road. The same money we would have made working at home, we instead made and spent on the road. While you don't have to do life this way, you can if you want.

***Time Tipping* helps you organize your life around the dream, not endlessly working toward it**—including helping you get paid in a way that supports your ideal way of life. If you could make money from anywhere, where would you go?

The thing is—even the rich have a hard time getting away. The freedom of expression of time is a factor in choosing your constraints.

For example, my companies include physical products, digital products, and concierge-level services. The industries I work in are traditional, but I operate them in a nontraditional way to intentionally create an environment and culture of time freedom. My projects vary from PROUDUCT, a global entrepreneurship solution making hundreds of unique products, helping businesses go from idea to market with full-service sourcing, product strategy, and end-to-end supply chain, to an international video editing service for creators, to executive coaching, consulting, online courses, speaking, blended learning, modular educational programs (self-directed learning courses, masterminds, podcasts, articles, keynotes, interviews, books, mentoring, university lectures), and more. Whether I'm home or abroad, I can get the work done from my cell phone while traveling with my family—*a positive reinforcing constraint I chose to keep myself mobile.*

I *Tipped Time* by using the principles you'll learn in this book.

While my random path is different from your random path—and there are no apples-to-apples comparisons—there is great love in sharing what works, what doesn't, and moving forward together. I hope you share what works for you too, with me and with those within your influence.

You can choose both meaning and money.

As I've traveled the globe visiting factories (factories where the products produced are likely in your home right now), I've seen the humanity in product creation and the inhumanity in remote office work, and I've seen people take control of their own lives while being responsible to their employer.

There are many ways to be productive, but there is only one of you. Taking care of yourself and attending to your priorities is personal. Become a pro at it.

Move from Distraction to Action

The four things you must know to help you implement the teachings from this book:

1. This is your book—your time, life, and decision to produce more space at your pace.
2. Treat the book like a toolkit and pull out the most appropriate tool for the occasion as the circumstances present themselves.
3. This is not a time-management book, for reasons you'll soon learn.
4. Your immediate application can produce a compound effect on your time, creating available space for more desirable possibilities than you originally imagined.

My hope in teaching *Time Tipping* principles has always been that people spend their newfound free time doing what they love with the people they love. Sometimes that happens. But I've found that sometimes people fill their newfound free time with more work. What's worthwhile to you is worthwhile.

> The moral of the anti-time management story is that the work you love can still be done without sacrificing time for something you love more.

Freedom is knowing you can work when you want and keep working if you wish to without being compelled. When you spend your time doing what you want and what you love, who's to say what's work and what's not?

The *Time Tipping Framework* is designed to help you make better decisions for greater alignment in your activities to create autonomy and set the ambience from the start. You'll discover how to think like a *Time Tipping entrepreneur*, be *time creative*, be *time inventive*, overcome *time distractions*, and create *time conversations* and *time actions* that inspire innovative answers to your professional and personal life goals.

Anti-Time Management will help you do the following:

» discover how to do the work now that will create the future you want without playing the victim to circumstance

» expand your problem-solving and leadership skills by creating space for aligned creativity to fill gaps and create gains

» become more inventive and innovative and challenge age-old limitations and constraints

» create and inspire a life of meaning at work, at home, and personally while creating a deep and wide positive impact for others

» shed self-destructive patterns and create self-constructive patterns to remodel your life and work according to your desired self-expression

» change the way you think, process, and share information about important topics to create desired results effectively

» reclaim your time and enhance your life and ability to contribute and serve others

Moving from distraction to action is a learned skill in thinking differently.

Get your free *Time Tipping Toolbox*
at RichieNorton.com/Time.

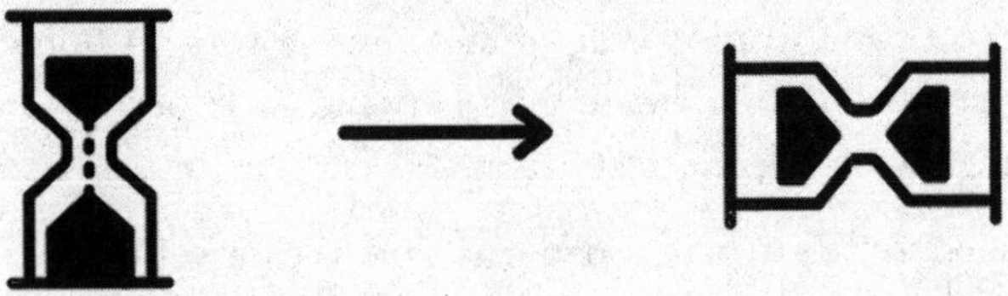

ANTI-TIME MANAGEMENT

INTRODUCTION
Why Anti-Time Management?

Time management is a seductive promise.

It sounds like you'll have more time if you apply the principles of time management. Yet . . . nothing could be further from the truth.

Why Do You Have Less Time Under Time Management?

The dictionary definition of the word *management* literally means "control." *Time management* means "time control." However, whose time is being controlled, by whom, and when is what matters to *Time Tippers.* Time management does not mean you have control over your time. Time management usually means your time is controlled by someone else.

Time management means
you don't have control of your time.

Let me be clear.

Time management has nothing to do with you controlling your own time.

Period.

Industry deliberately designed time management so a manager at work could control you and your time, what you do, where, and when.

Welcome to your *run-of-the-mill job.*

In fact, your vacation time, the hours you work, your breaks, when you retire (or not), and where and when you do your work—even if it's from home—are carefully calculated factors of time management (and often paired with a reward system of titles, roles, bonuses, employee of the month, and the like to enforce it).

Time management has great branding around it but doesn't live up to its promise.

Is it any wonder how people might manage their personal time using the professional time-management tools available to them only to end up with more work and less available time?

Your list of things to do does not need to be the same list as things to be done.

Under traditional time management, personal productivity is pernicious to professional productivity.

That means, under time management, the more available time you create means you have more work to be done! To top it off, time managers make sure it stays that way by design—counterproductively discouraging high producers.

The paradox of getting things done: the more you get done, the more is given to you to get done.

Traditional productivity management piles on more work without additional pay to workers. Excess capacity at work creates an efficiency tango between management and workers. Management tests employees to see how little pay they can bear and still get the job done. Employees test management to see how long they can stretch out work before they get fired.

What might effectively take one hour to get done could be *efficiently* cut up into tiny bite-size pieces and spread out over an entire day, week, month, or even *year*—requiring more managers to watch workers every step of the way.

Efficiency metrics can show improvements in productivity despite a lack of production.

Anti-time management looks at things differently.

Productivity (efficiency) and production (value conversion) are not necessarily the same thing. The formidable *efficiency dance* disappears when you stop wasting energy on things that don't matter. You can get things done and be done.

Traditional time management worked for its past designed purposes.

Virtues are virtues until virtues become vices.

Time management has become a vice.

Time management is a painful path to strive for autonomy and meaningful work because time management was not a tool designed to do that.

All Management Is Time Management

How the manufacturing term *time management* slipped into self-help mainstream vernacular is a mystery—unless, of course, industry realized they could be more efficient if employees could do better at managing their weekend time to increase the workweek output. *Lightbulb moment?*

Anti-time management helps you reclaim your time so you have a greater choice (and responsibility) in the matter of how you do life.

Time Management	Anti-Time Management
They Control Your Time	You Control Your Time

What controls your time more than any one person or system are the choices you make.

The consequences of your choices can either multiply or divide your available time.

Look, it's not wrong to be responsible and accountable to someone else for your time. Working together is key to getting great results. Working with employers, customers, or clients reliably throughout your career can and should bring you great purpose and joy. The key in your personal decision-making process at work and at home for greater autonomy is to remember that everything you agree to is a choice and so is its consequence—unintended consequences be damned.

When a consequence is viewed as a choice, you have a greater mental capacity to change your circumstances with different choices—even preemptively.

Own the amount of time you spend at work as a choice, not a consequence.

Don't play the victim of your job.

Hard work is a high.

Don't forget what you're reaching for while getting high on work.

As my mentor Stephen Covey would say, "When we pick up one end of the stick, we pick up the other end. Undoubtedly, there have been times in each of our lives when we have picked up what we later felt was the wrong stick." When you make a choice, you also choose its consequence.

The time consequences that come with your choices should be taken into consideration before you make decisions. In fact, in anti-time management, you proactively make decisions that actively free up your time now and in the future.

Time Management	Anti-Time Management
They Control Your Time	You Control Your Time
They Take Time	You Create Time

Time management takes up space. Anti-time management creates space.

Picture your calendar.

Traditional time management on a calendar might look like every hour of the day carefully planned out, full and blisteringly busy, no room for anything else, not even spontaneity, creativity, or heaven forbid a crisis—*unless it's planned.*

On the other hand, anti-time management might look like an open calendar because everything is already being handled.

Ironically, under time management, you may hear the familiar end-of-day cry, "*I was so busy, but I feel like I got nothing done.*"

However, with anti-time management, you may feel oddly productive and the day was breezy—even airy with available space for more. You may find yourself saying, *"I feel so lazy,"* even though you got that big thing done you had in store for the day—with room to breathe.

Of course, if you love calendaring, the anti-time management calendar would be filled with your ideal day, and you would love and fill every second of it.

Time Management	Anti-Time Management
They Control Your Time	You Control Your Time
They Take Time	You Create Time
They Took Your Space	You Create Space

Sometimes there is nothing more valuable than an empty calendar. Sometimes the key isn't filling the calendar. It's leaving it empty. Often a full calendar indicates an empty life.

At the end of the day, anti-time management is about owning your choices.

Time Management	Anti-Time Management
They Control Your Time	You Control Your Time
They Take Time	You Create Time
They Took Your Space	You Create Space
They Took Your Choice	You Make Choices

The fight for choice is a tale as old as time.

Freedom of choice is freedom of time. *Hasn't it always been that way?* Hasn't freedom largely been about your ability to choose how you spend your time and disallowing others from taking it from you?

How you spend your time is more important than how much you have.

Reclaim Your Time to Revolutionize Results

Time Tipping is simple to learn and apply—small changes make all the difference. If you want money, sell things. If you want a vacation, go. If you want art, make it. It's the *responsible* thing to do.

Here's how . . .

Time Tipping shows you ways to mitigate risk, stop waiting, and start living. *Time Tippers* build reliable processes around their purposes and learn how to integrate their dreams into everyday life—as opposed to those who endlessly tiptoe toward goals without ever actually achieving them. *Time Tipping* can be learned, shared, and put into practice to help make the best use of your time and create space to change your mind or change your course without stress.

This book aims to integrate relevant work-life principles for the next hundred years by advancing attention on time management to adapt aligned change with wise timing.

Time Tipping is for leaders, managers, entrepreneurs, and freelancers hungry to navigate the meaningful, productive new world of work. But it's not just for them. *Time Tipping* is for companies whose workforce, profitability, and growth strategy stem from people working remotely.

You'd think that corporations wouldn't appreciate disclosing anti-time management information like this in a book. Ironically, embracing these anti-time management principles helps organizations attract leadership and retain creative talent who work with purpose, understand data, and get desired results—no matter where they're from or where they live.

Time Tipping is for a whole new generation of workers in an always-on culture coming up in a working reality untethered from geography, for families wanting to spend more time together, and for individuals striving to live out their greatest aspirations.

Time is perhaps the most managed, controlled, incentivized, and gamified resource of all humankind throughout history.

Business is roughly a social experiment to see what can be done to increase desired outcomes by changing how time is managed and creates value. But today, it's not guesswork. It's precision—especially online. There's a term for it, *gamification*, and it's not necessarily a bad thing.

It's one thing to be in a game. It's another to be wholly unaware of the game being played around you. Your time can be gamified, and you can gamify your own time. *Time Tipping* identifies your intrinsic motivation to help you experience extrinsic rewards.

Many people don't have the opportunities you have. Your ideas, projects, work, and time can expand your impact deep and wide to create breakthrough opportunities for others.

How will you prioritize your attention?

Remote Time

If people lived forever:

Imagine the caveman who invented the wheel claiming his kids are lazy and entitled because they ride bikes.

Imagine the caveman who harnessed fire to cook claiming his kids are lazy because they use an oven.

Now, imagine a kid back in the day being asked by his dad to stand up from the couch and go change the channel on the TV by turning the dial.

Then imagine this same kid growing up and becoming a dad himself.

Now, imagine this dad has a remote control in his hand.

The dad asks his kid to get up off the couch and change the channel on the TV.

His son says, "But Dad, you have a remote control in your hand. You can just change the channel by clicking that button."

The dad looks at his son and instead of saying "Thanks!" and changing the channel, he sets the remote down and gives him a lesson on talking back, the value of hard work, calls him a derogatory name, and forces him to get up and turn the dial on the TV.

The only problem for the son is that . . . there is no dial on the TV anymore.

It's remote controlled.

That's the battle at work today—those with metaphorical remote controls who don't want to learn to use them are on the same projects as those who use the tech and are told they are lazy.

If we lived forever, would we change our ways, our ideas, our identities as we watched the world's technology change?

Whether you change the way you think and work or not, the world is changing around you. This new world provides both the opportunities you've always wanted and better ones you never imagined. You create your own world.

Make your time relevant to your dreams.

Let me emphasize:

Anything that can be done by a machine will be done by a machine. Your work will change to things that machines can't do—making human work more human. The same way you choose to spend your time on work today instead of washing your clothes by hand (like they still do in certain parts of the world where I've lived), the future of work will allow you to spend your time leveraging time doing work that machines don't do.

This is an era of leveraging the new rules and tools of work afforded by tech.

Of what use is *knowledge work* (a term coined by Peter Drucker back in 1959!) when all the knowledge in the world can be accessed instantly, but you don't know what information you need?

When knowledge lives in the cloud ubiquitously—*like time*—the personal responsibility for what you do with it is grave.

You have access to knowledge at a level unseen by any generation. A similar thing happened to the world and with a disintegration of power from the top with the invention of the printing press. It's a good thing. It's called transparency, trust, freedom, and independence. But you have to learn to read.

Automation does not automatically mean you have autonomy.

All the time in the world is only as meaningful to you as the meaning you attend to it instead of squandering it away.

Stop managing time. Start making meaning.

The remote past and distant future are like cymbals rhythmically crashing together, keeping the present's meaning on beat.

The timing couldn't be better.

You were born to mix it up.

The scales of time want to be tipped in your favor.

It's showtime.

ASK YOURSELF THESE SIX BASELINE QUESTIONS

I adapted these questions for your *Time Tipping* purposes directly from Alcoholics Anonymous for apparent reasons.

Instructions: Answer YES or NO

1. Have you ever decided to manage or "balance" your time better, but it didn't last?

   YES or NO

2. Do you ever envy people who can spend their time more freely than you?

   YES or NO

3. Have your time-management abilities (or lack thereof) caused trouble at home?

   YES or NO

4. Do you tell yourself you can stop working anytime you want to, even though you keep working even against your own expectations?

   YES or NO

5. Have you ever switched from one habit or program to another hoping that this would make you more efficient, effective, or successful?

   YES or NO

6. Have you ever felt like you *worked all day* and *got nothing done*?

   YES or NO

If you answered YES to any of these questions . . .

YOU ARE NOT ALONE

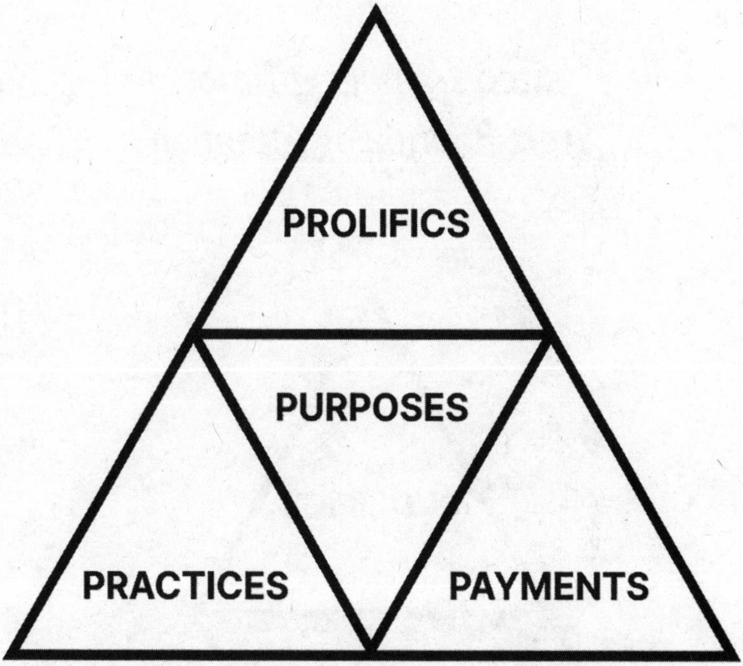
PROLIFICS
PURPOSES
PRACTICES
PAYMENTS

PART I
PURPOSES

Stop Managing Time,
Start Prioritizing Attention

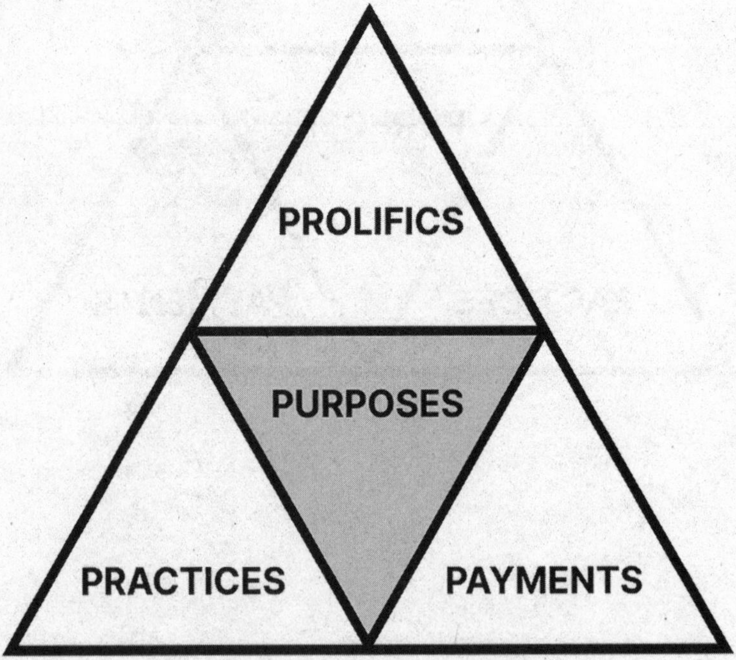

STOP MANAGING TIME, START PRIORITIZING ATTENTION.

MAKE FINAL CAUSE

YOUR FIRST CAUSE.

CHAPTER 1

Make Final Cause Your First Cause

How to Choose What to Do and When

It is vital that we are equipped with the humility to understand that changing the world and keeping innovation alive require that we change ourselves.

—WHITNEY JOHNSON,
bestselling author of *Disrupt Yourself*

Sirah spent much of her youth on the streets, homeless, in gangs, addicted, and abused. "I grew up with a medicine man, and we would sacrifice an animal, do a prayer around it, and eat it for like a month. There were some good skills that I gained, but there were a lot of weird things going down, a lot of sexual abuse, a lot of neglect," she told me. Growing up, she'd been kidnapped, raped, and left for dead more times than she'd like to remember.

Time and circumstance never were Sirah's friends.

"I dropped out of the fourth grade," she said. "I would have to go sell my Nintendo to get enough money for my dad to shoot heroin. . . . I was left alone for long periods of time." Her dad died of an overdose when she was young.

"I was just going through my report cards from school the other day," she told me. As her elementary school teacher reported:

> "Doesn't know how to connect with other children."
> "She's showing signs of not being cared for."
> "She's getting bullied as a result."

Sirah's life had been thrown into an out-of-control trajectory, until one day she did something that changed her fate.

Listen to This Voice

"I woke up at seventeen. There was this voice in my head that I thought was schizophrenia. And it said, 'You're not supposed to be living like this. This is not your life. This was a choice. You are supposed to be a rapper.' So I called my family, and I was like, 'Hey, guys, pretty sure I'm schizophrenic, but I'm going to go and listen to this voice.'

"I got sober. I got off of everything, and I went to go follow this voice."

So Sirah went down to Project Blowed, an open-mic hip-hop platform in South Central LA. She went every Thursday. At first, she just watched. But then, she rapped. She rapped badly.

Sirah was determined. She became what she thought she should become, and despite not knowing anything about being a rapper, she showed up where she could become one—and got booed offstage every Thursday.

Sirah explained to me:

> I'm the only girl, and I'm the only white person. I look out of my mind, and, honestly, looking back, I was. I freestyle every week, and I keep getting booed offstage because I am terrible. I mean, I am horrific, and I keep doing it. And so all these older rappers, they were called Freestyle Fellowship, and I love them dearly because they really changed my whole life. They were like, "Are you out of your mind? You're a little girl. You're white. Why do you keep doing this? You're bad."

> And my response was always, "Because I'm supposed to." Out of self-preservation, they came to me and said, "Okay, well, we're going to teach you how to rap because we have to suffer through you every week, and you keep getting booed offstage." So they taught me how to rap.

And they did—while also teaching her life skills she'd missed growing up.

One night, Sirah was invited to a party and met someone who threw shows and said he'd help her get onstage. She got her first show.

Sirah said, "And that show led to the next show, which led to the next show, which led to touring, which led to a message . . . from this guy named Sonny who wanted to work with me. . . . And when we met up, he ended up taking me in because I was homeless. We started recording into a broken laptop. Those songs turned into Skrillex's first song, 'Weekends,' which turned into 'Bangarang,' which turned into 'Kyoto.' All of us, just living in like a loft, a bunch of boys making music." Sirah and Skrillex (Sonny) won a Grammy for "Bangarang."

And that's how Sirah rose from homelessness to winning a Grammy.

When she received the Grammy, Sirah said, "Guys, this is a Grammy. This is really crazy. I am so grateful. When we started this, we were all living in a loft downtown. And then I moved into a garage in East LA with holes in the ceilings. So, this is beyond my wildest dreams. I don't even know if this is real right now. But I'm so grateful. I'm alive because of music, and I live to make music. So, thank you so much. Thank you to my family. *This is for you, Dad.* Thank you so much!"

She didn't have the opportunity growing up to learn any steps for behavioral change or goal setting or stage performance. Back then on the streets, no one was going to get her music lessons. She was never going to land an agent. There wasn't enough money to buy food or shelter, let alone promote a show. She'd never have enough. The achievement of the goal couldn't be at the end of next summer's music camp. There was no ten-year plan—she might be dead by then. It was now, or never.

Choose Your Response, Choose Your Future

Sirah's experience can teach many lessons about *life and time, struggle and success, character and courage.*

Sirah told me:

- "I get to choose what my past meant."
- "I get to choose what my past meant to create my future."
- "We have a choice in how we react."
- "Your reaction creates the energy around it."
- " . . . which is creating where I'm supposed to really be."

She continued:

> In the past six months, I got robbed by a bunch of people. Then I got my car stolen last week . . . but, you know what happened to me in the formative years of my life, that was not a choice. That was something that happened to me.
>
> The coolest thing is I get to choose how I perceive and label what is happening in my world. I spent a lot of time as a victim, but the most empowering thing I've realized is that I get to choose what my past meant. I get to choose what my past meant to create my future. The only choice I've really had in this whole thing is, okay, you've been wildly sexually abused and manipulated and psychologically tortured on some levels.
>
> You can either be a statistic . . . or you can go and be a survivor. You can be a pioneer; you can be a thought leader. You can be a visionary, you can be, you know, any and everything is our choice. And so when things happen, sometimes we don't have a choice about those events, but we do have a choice in how we react. . . . Your reaction creates the energy around it. I've found that my reaction to it creates the energy around it, which is creating the path to where I'm supposed to really be.

Your reaction—*your energy*—is in your control.

So is your time.

Turn the Scales of Time

The overwhelming joy of finally doing and being what you want and helping others do the same is unmatched. Like energy, your reaction to the outside world creates or takes your time, creating where you are, who you are, and who you want to be!

Changing or enhancing the direction of your life can be effectively lived around *identity and time* and *energy and action* in two distinct ways:

1. Decide who you want to be.
2. Act from that identity immediately.

Identity and Time: Sirah decided to become a rapper, now.

Energy and Action: Sirah embodied her new identity from day one, immediately.

Consider the timeline shift that happens in goal achievement, becoming the next best version of yourself and your ideal way of life just from these two statements:

1. *I want to be an artist.*
2. *I am an artist.*

The first statement puts the "goal" at the end of an unknown timeline. The second statement places the "goal" *squarely at the center* of everything you do—eliminating the goal and making life's choices an extension of the present. Showing up as *I want to be* is a totally different life (lifestyle, feeling, experience) than *I am*—two totally, completely different lives.

I want versus *I am* is a choice, not a destination.

When she started, Sirah wasn't a successful musical artist, but she had the courage to step onstage—arguably the last step in traditional performance preparation. The act of becoming what she wasn't ready to become changed her mindset, changed her behavior, changed her environment, and changed how she spent her time. In this newly created state, placing herself in the center of an adaptive ecosystem, mentors and other resources could finally come together to help—a cradle of maximum opportunity.

When Sirah moved her thinking to "I am," the ordinary *steps to success*—which would have otherwise taken *years* to climb—simply *disappeared.*

The opposite path to living her dream, of course, may have looked like endless wishing on a well-structured set of incremental, star-studded goal posts that would never align—full of hope and endlessly waiting in despair.

Traditional goal setting would have been a deterrent to Sirah. Yet how she self-identified moved her from distraction to action to traction—as it could be for anyone who has set a goal and not achieved it, *yet.*

Sirah gained control of her time and life by what Aristotle called *Final Cause—the sake of which a thing is done.*

If you were to meet Sirah today, you'd find her helping homeless teenagers overcome harsh realities, coaching celebrities through addiction, helping people heal mentally and spiritually, creating collaborative communities, environments, and events to improve the world, and, of course, making music.

To Sirah, *it's all music.*

Learn from Aristotle's Four Causes

The world is changed by people who aren't ready.

As it turns out, some of the greatest success stories never took a ladder climb or walked a mile in someone else's shoes before becoming who they wanted to become. Much of what we've learned about steps to success has come from those who never took them.

Aristotle proposed a theory we call the Four Causes to answer questions in nature and otherwise about *why* things are brought into existence.

Aristotle's Four Causes are Matter, Form, Agent, and Final. A classic example scholars use to describe the Four Causes is a dinner table:

1. It's made of wood (Material Cause).
2. It has four legs with a flat top (Formal Cause).
3. It was made by a carpenter (Agent or Efficient Cause).
4. It was built so people could have dinner together (Final Cause).

***Time Tippers* start with *Final Cause* to characterize the maximum effect of purposed time.**

Make Final Cause Your Only Cause

To Time Tippers:

The table is not the point—*the dinner is.*
The dinner is not the point—*the sake of the dining experience is.*
The experience is not the point—*the people are.*

. . . and so on.

Metaphorically, people will spend a lifetime building tables when all they had to do was order out.

So, what's the *real goal* of the dinner?

If this is a special dinner, who is it for, why, what kind of experience do we want to have, and how will the bonds of our relationships strengthen?

Do we need dinner at all to create the goal beyond the goal—Final Cause?

Could all this time and money spent on a table and dinner be spent differently to create an even better future by living a better present?

Or, maybe you want a family legacy table that will stand the test of time as an heirloom for the generations—a very different project and approach altogether.

Aristotle's Four Causes can help you understand the current trajectory of your life and how to change it to influence a better outcome—if you want.

In nature, Final Cause may help you understand how an oak tree starts as an acorn. But in time creation, your career, entrepreneurship, self-development, and happiness, Final Cause determines how you do everything—if you need to do anything differently at all.

So what's for dinner?

Next time you're hungry, forget the table. There are many ways to get full and countless places to eat. Unless the table is the goal, what's the real reason for dinner? Make *that* happen.

Transformations don't happen as transactions.

To implement *Time Tipping*, you need to decide if you're going to take the lead in your life with Final Cause or follow in the footsteps of others who didn't live the life you want to live.

What Are You Really Working For?

Final Cause lives beyond your goals—the sake for which you make goals in the first place. You don't work for work's sake. You work for something else.

Sure, you work for money, but what does that money buy? What do you spend your money on? Why? And so on.

Where do you hope all your work, hustling, saving, investing, and doing will land you and your loved ones?

When you picture your best future self, what is the state of things, and how do you experience this future?

What's the goal of the goal?

Is your dream fit for purpose?

Final Cause is the reason, the interest in why you do what you do, your hope for how things turn out—***how you imagine your best future***.

- Final Cause is more than the goal of the goal—it's the effectual living beyond the goal.
- Final Cause is the success after the success.
- Final Cause is the place where your time is spent on your values.
- Final Cause is where misaligned commitments are reexamined.
- Final Cause is purpose.

Final Cause thinking helps you integrate purpose into everything you do—even before you've finished the puzzle to your big-picture dream.

Puzzles are put together one piece at a time, not in one big block—and so are dreams. Final Cause helps you identify the big-picture dream, and *Time Tipping* helps you put together the oddly shaped interlocking pieces.

The mosaic of your dreams is made up of the small moments meaningfully pieced together.

Final Cause is your intangible expression of joyful living—that feeling of starting something new harmonizing with the fulfillment of accomplishment.

Are you sharpening pencils, or
are you creating art?

To *Time Tippers,* Final Cause is not the end—it's both the end and the beginning.

The end informs the beginning so you can begin living the values of the end from the beginning.

Dreams fall short of their purpose when you set a time-managed goal-path from means, not ends.

Living with purpose makes your dreams come within reach.

Entrepreneurs, for example, feel a sense of autonomy but lose freedom as they get busy following irrational time-sucking systems. No one is in business for business' sake. People are in business because their life is at stake. Work is meant to create the desired outcome. If your work is not creating the dream, what are you working on?

Your purpose is to have more time with your family, but your dream to be free will take five years. By then your thirteen-year-old child will be eighteen and out of the house. What do you do instead to get that freedom lifestyle you want here and now?

Bake your dream and available time to live that dream into your business model from day one.

Entertaining the idea of a new life is very different from doing the work to retain one.

Consider this:

- » Greatness becomes possible when we prioritize our purpose and integrate the expression of our values, now.
- » Our greatest future is found in not compromising our character along the way.
- » There's plenty of time to take yourself seriously—it's just usually never the right time. *Be kind to yourself.*

The reason entrepreneurs "don't have time" is because they build their business on those traditional *busy models* they tried to escape. Entrepreneurs have all the available time in the world if they build for available time and integrate available time from the start.

Current time-management hype would have you dangle the sake of your work (a carrot) dangerously at the end of a timeline (a stick) that you may never enjoy. Carrot chasing can keep you running but will also rob you mercilessly of your energy and time. Dreams inescapably rot right before your eyes when they hang from the end of a stick—forever in sight, but always out of reach.

Time Tippers start with the carrot. If you love carrots so much that you'll sacrifice the rest of your life chasing one, why not bake it into everything you do from the start? Did someone say carrot cake? (And yes, for Natalie's sake, the cake can be gluten-free, sugar-free, all the frees.)

Time Management	Time Tipping
Stick & Carrot	Carrot (Cake)

The fact is, too many people think they'll be able to sacrifice their time now to get more later *(time doesn't work that way)* only to find out that the systems they cemented over the years won't allow them to leave without things falling apart. This is a classic exit-strategy oversight.

Scalability inherently requires your functional ability not to be a bottleneck.

If you want more autonomy, why not code autonomy into the system?

Bake freedom of time into the process.

If the cake recipe calls for sugar in the list of ingredients, you put sugar in the bowl and mix before the cake is baked. If you don't, the cake will be baked with no sugar.

Time Tippers create autonomy the same way—from the start.

The *Time Tippers* recipe calls for your values to be mixed into your living now **before** doing your work. If you don't, the work will create an outcome that does not include your values.

- » If you want time, bake it in from the start.
- » If you want to live the sake of your goals now instead of forty years later in retirement, mix those values in now and watch your way of life rise as it bakes. *Forty years later, you'll have lived what could be considered multiple lives—a polymathic lifestyle.*

Mix your values into your daily living and find your voice, today. You can independently cause your purposeful process to begin. Don't compromise your priorities by hanging them like a carrot from a stick.

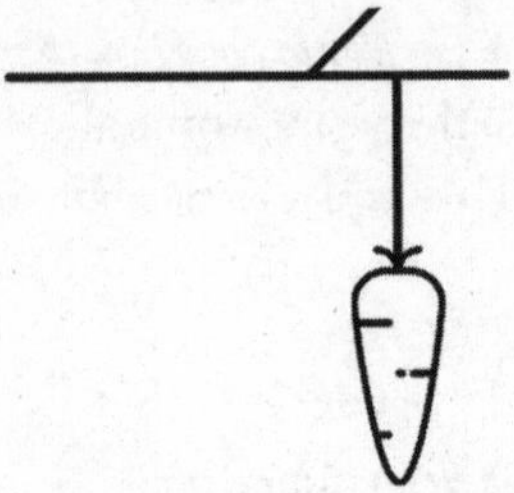

TIME MANAGEMENT

STICK & CARROT

TIME TIPPING

CARROT (CAKE)

If you want to reclaim your life,
start by reclaiming your time.

People will memorize and repeat their corporate values but forget their own.

It's irrational to think that a cake baked without sugar will come out of the oven filled with sugar. Likewise, it's illogical to think that a life lived at the sacrifice of priorities will one day show up as a prioritized life.

Of course, you can change your life. You can turn it around. You can end one thing to start another. Don't fool yourself into thinking that what you're doing now is creating something it won't.

Compromising values now as a choice and thinking it will enhance your ability to live your values later is irrational.

I spent a day teaching chief executive officer (CEO) millionaires making from around $1 million a year to well over $50 million a year how to get their lives back. I straight up told them they had no excuse. When you cement systems of operation, you can't get out . . . even when you get to the top.

It's a myth to think you can escape the grind before learning to live in the present. How you get paid is more important than how much when it comes to work-life flexibility. Exits are great, but it's better to do it as a choice, not a consequence of lousy modi operandi.

Living your values now, as a choice, fortifies *Time Tipping* as a productive pattern that will enhance your ability to continue to live your values later with greater expansion.

Not only is it possible to bring Final Cause into your life now, but doing so creates the fertile environment and the adaptive culture for everything you want to be and do to happen sooner than later, if not immediately.

If you align your future point of view with today's point in time and give yourself space to live that experience now, you won't have to save your dreams for later.

Don't save your dreams—dreams melt like ice cream.

Time well spent on dreams today pays dividends of more well-spent time later.

As a *Time Tipper*, you're investing time and collecting time, all the time.

Higher-Order Thinking: From Goals to Meta-Goals to Final Cause

What to do next:

Goals. **Choose a goal that eliminates most problems.** Every goal comes with a set of problems. Ask yourself why you have a certain goal in the first place. What is the job of that goal? How can you accomplish the job of the goal in a way you enjoy sooner than later? Ask interesting questions that make room for a variety of perspective-shifting answers.

Meta-Goals. **Move your point of view beyond the goal to your categorical desire—the meaning or purpose beyond the goal.** This thought process shifts what it takes to realize the big picture by opening various new goal possibilities (means) to reach the bigger picture. Creative problem solvers look beyond the tools they have and *don't* have (goals are tools to reach a bigger-picture dream) to find other ways to get the result they want with different means and timelines.

If the current goal is to hike a mountain, perhaps the meta-goal is to enjoy that feeling of the view from the top. With the meta-goal in mind, that means you could potentially take any route you want up the mountain or get there any way that is most enjoyable—from hiking to climbing to driving to a helicopter ride. (As an aside, I suggest taking the Gornergrat Railway if you're at the Matterhorn and looking for a leisurely ride.) Of course, if the goal is the hike itself, then there's no complaining when your neighbor gets there faster on the back of a mule.

Final Cause. **Rescue your meta-goal from the ledge of your long-distance timeline and bring it home by placing it directly at the center of your life. Act from your future, not toward it.**

This time, instead of putting your dreams on the periphery, place them at the center. Work from your goals, not toward them. You can rescue your dreams from the end of a timeline by simply moving them to the front of the line. You can't wait for dreams because they are not active. Dreams don't wait for you either because dreams are not patient.

It's 100 percent easier to increase your time and freedom by eliminating the dumb things you do every day than to try to be 100 percent more productive doing more dumb things.

Behavioral consistencies can be future driven and future paced for better or worse.

Find joy in growth. Imagine the steps you envision working toward a goal instead of from it. Saying to yourself *"I will"* versus *"I am"* immediately generates a very different decision-making process. For example, saying *"I will run regularly"* can put you in over-preparation mode. However, the statement *"I am a runner"* can get you into running shoes and onto the trail. Telling yourself *"I will retire one day and do XYZ"* (toward the goal) becomes a very different life from *doing XYZ today and building a career around it to support it* (from the goal).

Living values in the present looks like caring enough to *make decisions from your values, not toward them,* by *creating a culture around being* (and helping others become along the way).

APPLY THIS EXAMPLE TO YOUR GOALS

If the purpose of writing a book, for example, is to get speaking gigs, you can speak now without waiting for the book. In fact, speaking may enhance the credibility and writing of the book itself. Goals can be interchangeable or rearranged. The switchability of goals using higher-order thinking is important to eliminate unnecessary time-effort.

However, what's the purpose of your future speaking gigs? Is it to sell a product, make impact, or "be" a speaker? You can compress your goals instead of separating them.

Could a speaking gig be recorded and transcribed into a short book and leveraged to gain market awareness and sell products to your audience based on the questions they ask based on your content? Yes.

Keep thinking through your goals to the job your goals are supposed to accomplish. The more steps (goals) you can eliminate, the more missteps you will avoid.

Living life from Final Cause creates a different mode of operation that almost looks opposite to waiting, pushing, and chasing that same dream way out there.

Make money. Don't chase money.
Make dreams. Don't chase dreams.
Making > Chasing

Meta-goals at the center of your time create a naturally expansive life in all areas of living as opposed to a compartmentalized lane that may or may not lead you to where you want to go.

In spirit, you become it before you become it. A seed already has a tree in it.

Final Cause is the seed.

Identify Final Cause with the Four-*P*s of Productivity

Many leaders, managers, executives, entrepreneurs, parents, teachers, *even time-management consultants* (heaven forbid!) start projects to free their time only to create a new prison of time. *Living from Final Cause will help you move from prisons of time to prisms of time.* There is no autonomy when bulleted lists become prison bars.

For the past twenty years, I've been interviewing millionaire and billionaire executives, creators with millions of subscribers and followers, famous authors, amazing parents, grandparents, great-grandparents, entrepreneurs, adventurers, founders, venture capitalists, investment bankers, doctors, therapists, lawyers, and even the top consultants, coaches, athletes, farmers, world leaders, and educators on the planet and more and more and more. I've been asking the question about work-life balance and documenting their experiences. I've gone into the depths of world-renowned research of the past two centuries of "modern management" (and beyond) to learn what we currently know about time management, productivity, happiness, regret, and human flourishing.

Guess what I found? The most "successful" people may be *more* clueless about "work-life balance" than everyday people. It makes sense. They didn't find the answer to balance in their wealth or fame. In fact, many successful people regret how they've spent their days.

Goals, habits, strengths, personality tests, time management, and more are a means to an end—moving beyond the means and into their meaning is where *Time Tipping* begins.

Successful people often regret not gaining the ability to take control of their personal time and their personal relationships. People regret missing their chance. However, people don't regret life-work flexibility, agility, and the ability to work and live meaningfully. Take a chance on worthwhile pursuits that engage your mind, energize your life, and strengthen relationships.

Goals, habits, and strengths are a mere means to an end—don't let them be ends unto themselves. Give yourself space to outgrow your expectations—give yourself room to breathe—by acting from Final Cause. You may have been stuck in the hamster wheel of to-do lists and time management for so long that you find it near impossible to think about a life of variety, an abundant future, or whatever a rich life might mean to you.

Begin with the transformational power of Final Cause. People often ask me, "What should I do?" I reply, "You'll know what to do when you know who you want to become."

Don't set traditional goals. Instead, prioritize meaning before means. Create an environment with the essence and impact of the goal before you have the means. Meaning informs means. Your mind is the first environment to prepare.

The life you have in mind will surely turn out different than you imagine. So what? Life is crazy. We first create in the mind and then in the world.

Strategy is in the head. Tactics are in the hands. Results are in the heart.

IDENTIFY YOUR FINAL CAUSE

Start *Tipping Time* by identifying Final Cause in your Life with the Four-*P*s of Productivity:

1. Personal
2. Professional
3. People
4. Play

I work through questions like these with clients to help them reprioritize their attention to improve their approach to achieve their chosen results (or something better) sooner than later. This activity helps you put your priorities (Final Cause) at the center of your life, not on the fringe.

Using the exercise has helped me make significant career changes, housing moves, financial decisions, and intentions around how I spend my time with Natalie and our children individually and together. I use the Four-*P*s of Productivity weekly, monthly, or whenever I want to re-center my life.

This activity will also help you move from distraction to action and set you up for aligned anti-time management projects through the *Time Tipping* model. We're taking a holistic look at what you're trying to accomplish and how you'd ideally like to show up in the world so you can align your time investments.

Ask Yourself These Three Final Cause Questions

Question 1: What are important things to you that you want to do *now* that keep coming back to your mind?

Question 2: What are important things to you that you've been putting off until *later* that you want to do *to feel* like you can live a life *without regret*?

Question 3: What kind of *character traits* do you want to embrace to become the person you want to be over the next two or three years to *feel productive* with your growth?

Apply These Three Questions to Each of the Four-*P*s

These are prompts to help you think through the questions, but the activity is not limited to these questions. Be creative. Take time with this. Have your significant other (personal or professional or both) identify their Four Purposes. It's okay if you and your significant other(s) have different priorities around your purposes. You're different people. Your aim is to understand the aspirations of one another and support each other. In this way, even if your ambitions are different, supporting each other puts you on the same page and allows you to create purposed time for each other together and respectively to live Final Cause.

PRIORITIZE YOUR PURPOSE

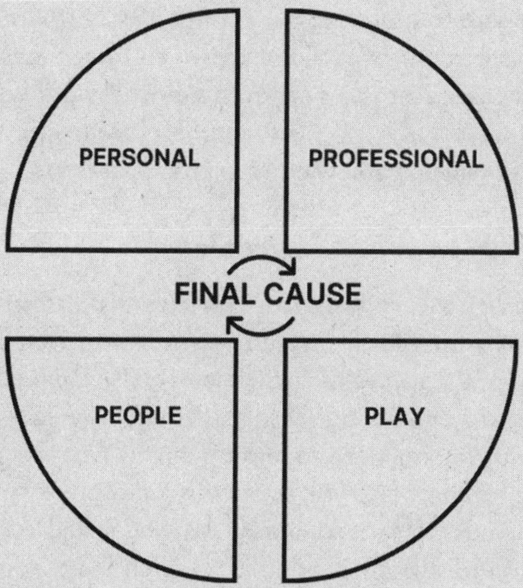

1. Personal

Personal Purpose relates to priorities that would be just for you. These are priorities involving *only* you. This could include everything from your health to your spirituality to maybe just some personal-growth goals that you've been thinking about for a long time, anything that revolves around your person, anything that you would want to do just for yourself. These could be educational aspirations. Anything that develops you on a personal level is fair game. What are the things you can't put out of your mind?

2. Professional

Professional Purpose relates to priorities that could include any accomplishments related to your career. This could consist of promotions or recognition you would like to receive. They could also be monetary objectives. How much money would you like to make in your current job? Or, if you're (becoming) an entrepreneur, how much money would you need to make a month to maintain your current lifestyle? What are your financial aspirations over the next two to three years? What is it professionally that you need to make your work worth your time and to feel alive, engaged, and happy with your contribution? What value do you want to create for others?

3. People

People Purpose relates to priorities around important people in your life. If I were doing this exercise right now, I would write the names of family members. I would put in business partners' or associates' names. Perhaps I would put in some people with whom I need to make amends. Whatever people or relationships come into your mind, write down their names, and then write next to each something that you would like to do for that person to strengthen your relationship. I've tried to choose things that these people are interested in, instead of my own interests, and support them in that. Your show of support can look like a text message, a date, time set aside, a trip, and so on. Truly, in my opinion, the People Priorities are the most important and the most difficult to maintain. Relationships are dynamic. Take the time to make the time for the relationships around you. In the end, few things matter, and relationships are the few things.

4. Play

Play Purpose relates to priorities, activities, and contributions that fill your soul and make you feel energized. Many people get into business to free up their time, but then they never do anything with that time. People get into business for themselves so they can free up their time to travel the world, spend more time with their family, do service, and go on mission trips. Let's take the first step to make those dreams a reality and write them down. Whatever you want to do, put down the things that would help you enjoy life more. It could be anything. Play Priorities should be the things that you think will make you feel happy or energized. Write down things that contribute to your mental wellness or serve others to make their lives a little better. What do you do when you're done with work? Or rather, what would you like to do ideally when you're done working? What do you want to do in retirement? Would you like to do that now? Put that down. Are there certain places you've always wanted to go? What's something that you'd like to look forward to? Put that down.

5. Choose One

Look back at your life's dreams under the Four-*Ps*. Can you do all of them at once? The reality is you probably can't do them all at the same time.

- Look at your Personal List, Professional List, People List, and Play List.

- If you could keep only one dream from each list, which ones would they be?
- Circle the one thing you'd keep from each list.

You should have Four Priorities to support your Four Purposes in front of you now.

Congrats!

What you've just done, the majority of the world has never, ever done. They have all these ideas in their head, all things in their minds that they would like to do, but they keep telling themselves, "I can't, I can't, I can't," or get overwhelmed. They can't prioritize.

In just a matter of minutes, you have gone from having all these ideas in your head and boiled them down to the four most important things to you in your life right now. Seriously, give yourself a hug, a round of applause, whatever it is. What you have just done is huge.

If you did this exercise right, you have all of your hopes and dreams written in one place, and you've distilled them into the Four Priorities of Final Cause.

What are the chances that the rest will come together if you focus on these top Four Priorities?

These Four Purposes and Priorities are your North Star for now. Whenever you have to navigate through the rough waters of important decisions, you can ask yourself what choice will bring you closer to making living your priorities happen or pushing them further away.

Keep these Four Purposes and supporting Four Priorities in mind throughout this book to create a strategic and tactical work plan with these purposes (Final Cause) at the center of your life.

As you do so, your Professional Priorities will support your Personal Priorities and provide the space you need to reclaim your time and life.

You can do this exercise again and again as you realize your dreams or as they change. If you decide to do something that leads you further away from a Final Cause Priority, you're now able to make that choice intentionally (not haphazardly) because your priorities changed.

6. Make It Happen

Write down your Four Final Cause Priorities.
Write down the date you want to accomplish each one.
Write down what you're going to do to create an environment at home and work so the space you live in encourages behaviors aligned with your values.
Write down an if-then statement for each of your Four Priorities.

For example, if your Personal Priority is to be fit, your Professional Priority is to make a million dollars, your People Priority is to improve your relationship with a loved one, and your Play Priority is a trip around the world with your family, here's a blanket formula you can use (or create your own) to write an if-then statement that keeps you centered:

If I do <u>ABC</u>, then I'll achieve <u>XYZ</u> by <u>DATE</u>.

You can take it a step further toward the meta-goal—the reason beyond the goal—to keep you motivated like this:

If I do <u>ABC</u> <u>every day</u>, then I'll achieve <u>XYZ</u> by <u>DATE</u>, so that <u>HAPPY THING happens years before I'd imagined</u>.

What you've just done is inverted your timeline. Many of our priorities are simply not prioritized. By moving priorities from the fringe of your timeline (where "someday" lives) and putting them at the center of your life (where you are right now), your priority-achievement timeline is inverted. This inverse timeline, or reverse chronology, helps you eliminate unnecessary steps and act on the right ones.

You can get even more "meta" by reversing the order of the if-then statement or removing parts of the statement altogether and operationalizing even deeper into the *Time Tipping Methodology*. Like this:

> I'm living my HAPPY THING now because with *Time Tipping*, I found that all the steps I thought it would take to get here *were totally unnecessary*.

This statement may not work for every situation. Still, it is undoubtedly true in many situations—or at least a statement like this can help you evaluate whether what you're waiting for is necessary *versus* your fear of just stepping up.

7. Crush Fears

Every time I teach these principles, someone tells me it can't be done because of reason after reason. I'll also hear stories about how this is only for people who have certain resources or in certain situations. These critics are right for two reasons: every situation is different, and if you don't believe you can, you're right. But for you, reading this book, you have no excuse. For your purposes, no time, no education, no experience, and no money are no excuse. Begin where you are. Don't tell yourself you need "more" before you start.

Your job as a *Time Tipper* is problem-solving through creativity. Also, as you'll learn, you don't have to solve all of your own problems, but experts can—that's called *Expert Sourcing*.

If you hear yourself telling yourself you can't do it for various reasons, consider asking yourself a new question:

> What can I do to overcome ABC, without XYZ happening, by DATE?

And:

Who can help me overcome ABC, without XYZ happening, by DATE?

Or:

If these problems were already overcome, what would be done next?

Because:

When I am living on purpose, my priorities align.

FOUR-*P*s OF PRODUCTIVITY

WHAT	WHY
PERSONAL	IF THEN
PROFESSIONAL	IF THEN
PEOPLE	IF THEN
PLAY	IF THEN

FOUR-*P*s OF PRODUCTIVITY

WHAT	WHY
PERSONAL PRIORITY	DATE FEAR AND OBSTACLES TO OVERCOME
PROFESSIONAL PRIORITY	DATE FEAR AND OBSTACLES TO OVERCOME
PEOPLE PRIORITY	DATE FEAR AND OBSTACLES TO OVERCOME
PLAY PRIORITY	DATE FEAR AND OBSTACLES TO OVERCOME

Get Your Free Download of the Four-*P*s of Productivity Worksheet and Other Anti-Time Management Tools at RichieNorton.com/Time.

WORK FOR FLEXIBILITY, NOT BALANCE.

CHAPTER 2

Work for Flexibility, Not Balance

How to Own Your Time

> Too often, we forget that our professional lives can, and should, be joyful.
>
> —DORIE CLARK, bestselling author of *Stand Out*

Doug started working for a very large US investment bank in New York City. He worked in highly quantitative groups but stood out for communication, problem-solving, and interpersonal skills. This led to quickly increasing both his income and his responsibilities. Ultimately, Doug got a large promotion to managing director and was asked to relocate from New York City to Paris with his family.

Doug said, "We jumped at the chance to live internationally and have our young kids learn a second language. But here's the thing—promotions at investment banks are like pie-eating contests where the first-place prize is more pie. Not only do you have to *love* pie, but pie is the *only* thing you can love. While I had more responsibilities, it didn't always come with more resources, and the hours and scope were unrelenting."

He continued, "There's a morbid joke within the industry that the job is a golden cage—the pay, prestige, etc., look amazing to those on the outside, but for the people in the job, it is indeed a cage and lifestyle that most can't break free from. Lifestyle creep happens, your ego gets involved, and suddenly you are as dependent upon the paycheck as a drug addict is to heroin.

"Growing up a child of teachers," he said, "we never had a lot of disposable income and were taught the value of saving and planning. Going into the finance industry, I thought I was changing the future for my kids. I saved, saved some more, and prioritized frugality. I would justify the long hours and the sacrifice I was making as doing it *for* my kids and family. What I didn't realize was what it was *doing* to them."

REFLECT: While your situation is different, how do the following statements from Doug ring true to you?

Doug described his situation to me like this:

» "The hours away from the family were tremendous."

» "We had always been a very close-knit family, but my kids were going through challenges learning French and adapting to a new country."

» "I found myself so busy with this opportunity that I didn't even notice the toll it was having on them."

» "I'd leave before they went to school and come home just in time to say good night."

» "Sundays were for catching up on the work and email that didn't fit in from Monday to Friday."

» "When I was around my family, the stress made my mind so cluttered and preoccupied, I might as well have not been present at all."

» "I was 'successful,' but I didn't have control."

- "I didn't have control of my time."
- "I didn't have control of my priorities."
- "I didn't have control of when or where I worked."
- "I didn't have control of my time off."
- "I didn't even have control of my health due to lack of time."

Doug knew that if something was to change, he needed to change. He wanted to live life more on his terms. He wanted more time with his family. He wanted to be able to take the kids to school, to hear about their day, to help them with homework. He wanted to be able to take vacations. He wanted to live where he wanted to live. He wanted to have time for hobbies. He wanted to have time for his spouse, for date nights, and for random adventures. He wanted time just to have fun. He wanted to have time to work out. He wanted time to cook meals for the family. Doug dreamed of doing all this "while still making an income and having an impact on people."

He figured he couldn't be the only person struggling with this, so he turned to books and podcasts on personal development. That's when Doug discovered my work and reached out to me. He was in Paris with his family during a government shutdown and wanted to learn about mobility, work-life flexibility, and "being the engineer and architect" of his own life.

How Would You Answer the $800,000-a-Year Question?

"In the middle of our coaching," Doug said, "I had one of the most pivotal moments in my working life. I was getting a lot clearer on my priorities and the future I wanted to create for myself and my family." He continued:

> Just then, I received a call from one of my old bosses from when I started working in finance. He had just started a new, much bigger role managing hundreds of people, and he needed someone to help him. Someone to run a large

and critical department that was suffering in morale, needed to be upskilled and internally marketed better. He couldn't think of a better person for the role and wanted to know if I was interested. The role would be back in New York City and would come with $800,000 (USD) in total compensation.

Was I in or was I out? $800,000 is an enormous sum of money. I had an incredible moment of clarity and said to myself, "That role isn't for me—I want to say no, and I will say no without regret because it isn't offering me what I most desire." It wasn't that I didn't value $800,000 or that $800,000 wasn't a lot of money to me. It's that I asked myself different questions and had different priorities.

Doug reasoned within himself from the point of view of Final Cause—his ultimate purpose:

» "What comes with this $800,000? What is my day-to-day going to look like?"

» "I could physically feel in my bones the daily commute, getting to the office before sunlight, fighting the internal politics all day, and staying until after dark. The pang of missing more time doing something more fulfilling."

» "I knew the trade-off was even more stress, even more time away from family, even less time for any personal hobbies, and that my health would suffer."

» "I would blink, and the kids would be grown and I would've missed it."

» "I realized that I only had a handful of summers with them before they left the house and started lives of their own. The small number of summers with them was eye-opening and motivating to me."

Regarding his decision, Doug explained, "For me it was a no-brainer to say no, but I also surprised myself with how clear and resolute I was about it. I was nervous about how to tell my first boss and mentor no for a new job he was clearly excited about and himself was willing to sacrifice for."

Practice practical duality. When Doug told me about the $800,000 opportunity he was turning down, I worried. I didn't tell him I was worried, but I wanted to understand more about his intent and the life he was picturing. I thought of his family and wondered about Doug's decision to turn down such a lucrative offer—one that his younger self would have leaped at in a second. I asked him several questions, and when I felt like I understood his purpose, I asked if I could share some unconventional ideas with him.

We talked through the choice between money and meaning and how they don't have to contrast. Money and meaning can complement each other through creativity.

In *Time Tipping*, the choice between two good options is considered not divisive but an opportunity for *practical duality.* *Practical duality* is a term I coined to help think through important life choices and problem-solve by blending two contrasting aspects of work and life together—like a photographer's use of light and shadow.

Build trust through difficult conversations. I didn't want Doug to miss out on the opportunity of a lifetime, and I wanted to respect his experience and values. So I shared with him something I'd learned from Stephen M. R. Covey, who had taught me that when there is a difficult conversation, ask yourself how you can have that conversation and still build trust.

How can you have a difficult conversation and build trust?

When Doug explained that he didn't want the job because he didn't want his time taken away, we had a discussion about ways he could propose to make it work now or in the future without having his time taken away. The objective was to increase trust and transparency in the relationship with his old boss, whom he respected deeply. We came up with happy alternatives around results-based work that would be valuable to his boss that he could propose that also maintained Doug's autonomy.

Doug said, "I had an incredible perspective shift, which was that you could say no in such a manner which builds trust and sets you up for potential consulting in the future, which could be done on a project basis from anywhere. The consulting twist is something that never occurred to me. To me, the only thing that was on the table was this job full-time in a location that I didn't want. My eyes were opened to the fact that my answer didn't need to be a yes or no—that I could add my own answer in the form of consulting on my terms in the future."

Doug used the difficult conversation to build trust and simply told his old boss the truth. Doug told him that he was honored he was thinking of him and that his old boss needed someone who was going to commit 150 percent. While the work itself would be fascinating, he wasn't willing to give up all the things that went along with what would be required in the job. He told him his next role would be one where he could pick the projects and clients he works with, where and how he lives, and have more flexibility between his work and life.

"To my surprise," Doug described, "he completely understood (and wrestles with this as well himself), and we left it open that in the future there'd be consulting projects he would need my expertise on. This episode was a huge test for me personally."

Doug had always wondered about starting his own firm. Now, his old boss could potentially become his first major client.

Doug said:

> It's incredibly easy to say what you value. It's another thing to be tested on it. I was telling myself that I valued family, that I valued flexibility, that I valued working toward being location independent. But how would I respond when a very high-profile, big-prestige, and large compensation package was offered which went against what I thought I valued and wanted to move toward? Would I waver and say, "Just a couple of more years"? Making this commitment to my values and 'passing this test' gave me even more confidence to move toward our dream of living life on our own terms.

Create Time Tipping Projects. Doug and his wife, Lindsey, an occupational therapist, invested time into developing her online business so that her income could grow and they could ultimately be location independent. They developed high-end programs for occupational therapists looking to build, grow, and scale their own private pay practices. Location freedom was important to them, but when they dug deeper they found that what they really wanted was time freedom and flexibility. Time freedom to them meant being able to choose how much and when they worked. The actual by-product of that would be location freedom.

Choose a critical restriction. "If we want to go to Japan for eight weeks during the summer holiday," Doug said, "I want to be able to say yes without hesitation. This gives us a critical restriction. It means we must be smart and resourceful about the types of projects we consider but, more important, how we go about executing them."

Ask questions to distinguish positive constraints. Here are some questions they asked to reverse engineer their purposes for daily living that you can adapt to your situation:

- "What activities can I say yes to, but, more important, what does that mean I should be saying no to?"
- "Is there a different way to do this project that gives us time back?" (This has led to hiring virtual assistants and subject-matter experts on a project-by-project basis. At our core, we put a lot of focus on batching and automation.)
- "What videos, blogs, interviews, and recordings can be done in advance?"
- "How can we get 'ahead' of ourselves during the school year so that we are largely off work in the summer?"
- "How can we structure the calendar of our launches such that the coaching calls don't fall during critical family time?"

Beware of liberating yourself into captivity. *Time Tipping* happens when constraints create freedoms that prevent future negative chain(s) of events.

Did they get it perfect?

"No, not yet," he said. But they've made incredible progress and are continually adapting. He added, "Better than perfect is the confidence and realization that this is actually under our control." They get to decide what's right for them and then do the hard work to make it a reality.

Doug reflected, "Before, I think we were just letting life happen to us—we were taking things as they came. But now we have a much more focused intention. We have a target we are shooting for rather than continually dodging things."

Choose work-life flexibility, not balance. "This summer we worked for eight weeks from Portugal, which was magical. The kids were in different camps such as surfing, tennis, and robotics each day. We explored the entire country, starting in the South and picking up and moving about every week or two until we made it up north close to Spain. We went from blue beaches studded with cliffs to green mountains dotted with vineyards to small towns where locals spent all day on a winding river."

Become available for life's tender moments. "Lindsey's mother recently passed away," Doug said.

> She traveled back to the US for seventeen days to be with her dad. It is always stressful to lose a parent no matter who you are or your situation. For those seventeen days, my wife focused on helping her dad. Due to the changes we'd made, I was able to be fully present with our children. I was 100 percent available to them.
>
> And it just so happened that we had already built out our program for occupational therapists (all automated) that

was taking place during her actual visit and sales were coming in automatically, and we made thousands of dollars while she was helping her dad—all due to preplanning and being prepared.

As I write this, Doug and Lindsey and their children are planning to move to Portugal and work remotely on their respective projects because they've practiced a life that is location flexible. Doug said, "There's a ton of things to sort out, but given the strides we've made in engineering our life and business, we know that not only can we figure this out, but we also have the time to do so as well."

Time collapses when something you thought takes a hundred steps to achieve takes only one.

Seek Work-Life Flexibility, Not Work-Life Balance

Balanced forces create unchanging motion. Seeking balance between life and work is like playing tug-of-war or trying to open a door while someone is holding it closed.

Changing motion requires unbalanced force—push or pull. Trying to balance your time between life and work keeps you stuck because balanced forces are motionless. Life is tugging on one side, and work is tugging on the other.

If you want forward motion in the direction you want to go to create positive change, then your responsibility is to set things in motion (not do it all). Naturally, you need to *unbalance* your life, but get the ball rolling in the direction you'd like to go (and change direction when you want). Life and work can support one another with alignment and elasticity of time. Work-life flexibility minimizes stress and maximizes advantages because it helps you win the game of tug-of-war (or avoid it altogether) and opens doors.

Time Tippers seek work-life flexibility, not work-life balance.

Several years ago, a college student named Benjamin Hardy emailed me. He had read my book *The Power of Starting Something Stupid* and wanted to connect. We jumped on a consulting call, and I taught him how to execute his goal to become a successful writer. With remarkable speed, he went on to become a successful blogger. From there, he transformed his blogging platform into a business, one that fitted his ideal lifestyle and was aligned with his overarching goals. Within seven days of receiving monetization feedback based on his desired lifestyle, Ben earned $21,000, which he wrote about on his Inc.com blog.

However, becoming a successful writer wasn't his real goal. Ben wanted to write to influence people for good throughout his lifetime while caring for his growing family right now. At the time, Ben and Lauren had just taken in three foster children while Ben was still in school and trying to make ends meet. Ben had a challenging upbringing and was eager to learn how to change the trajectory of his life and help others along the way.

Ben is now a bestselling author. He's making seven figures running a business that he designed around prioritizing his ideal lifestyle by identifying overarching personal and professional goals. Ben applied the principles of *Time Tipping* and lives a life most people postpone until retirement (if ever). He has the luxury of working only after he's put his paramount life values—his family and his faith—on his calendar first.

Ben began with Final Cause and then unbalanced his life in the direction he wanted to go with priority projects around his end purposes. He knew what mattered to him personally and professionally—but the needle moved when he moved his goal from a *future when*, at the end of a distant timeline, to *now*. As Dr. Benjamin Hardy says, "Success is achieved by being true to your future self."

Purpose is resilient.

**Making time for what you want is an art—
you hold the paintbrush despite the canvas.**

Make What Matters Matter Now

Time Tipping demonstrates how two people with the same job, earning the same income, can achieve significantly different outcomes in their lives—one enjoys little or no freedom of time, while the other seems to have *all the time in the world.*

How do two people with basically the same job lead such different personal lives?

Bobby (in his midthirties) has a wealthy father (in his late sixties). Bobby's father recently lamented to him his life's plan. His life plan was to work hard and become wealthy enough to eventually have more time available for his family. In retrospect, Bobby's dad now realizes that he lost time with his family for years because he was too busy working. Filled with regret, he cautioned his son not to follow in his footsteps.

Instead of missing out on thirty years of life with his family, Bobby's father could have held the same job, earning the same amount of money, and also enjoyed the family time he so desired *the entire time*. But no one taught him how. No one in his life modeled a different way of life.

Your priorities may be in order while your life is totally out of order.

Work and life shouldn't just be flexibility-focused. Work and life should be congruency oriented.

What you spend your time on now is what matters to you now.

It's not always about changing what you prioritize
but how and when you make priorities matter.

Prioritizing Final Cause crowds out distractions and makes time for traction.

Even if you think you're working for some bigger payoff later, what you're doing now matters—*that's how you show up to others.* If it doesn't matter, or if it's of lesser importance, why are you still doing it? Time seems so abundant—like the future is everlasting—so we have the tendency to take time for granted.

Time Tippers prioritize ideals today and create a flexible hybrid of work-life living as support now.

***Time Tipping* is winning the battle of awareness, alignment, and attention.**

The Billionaire with No Time

I met a billionaire who was recently widowed. She told me her husband had no "work-life balance," *no time* for his family, and what a terrible father it made him. *He was no stranger to time-management practices.* He'd made his money building a business managing thousands of employees' time from the ground up. According to his family, he hadn't managed to make time for them.

The time-sucking, distracting, linear march of postindustrial time management is irrelevant and obsolete when it comes to your personal life.

It's not as much about what you do as it is who you become in the process.

***Time Tipping* makes more time in the long term than it takes in the short term.**

Create Space to Fill the Void

The *paradox of time management* is that absurd personal discovery when the more you manage your time, the less time you have for your most important things, and the less you manage your time, the more you get done.

It takes courage to create a new timeline for your life.

Prioritize Your Attention on Aligned Projects

By and large, humans aren't that good at predicting the future. So we plan out extensive (almost innumerable steps) that are unnecessary before doing what it takes to tip the scales of our dreams in our favor.

Align purpose to establish priorities
and create projects for work-life flexibility.

While people are better at identifying patterns of success than predicting the future, we tend to choose paths that are *barely* correlated to our dreams instead of actions directly causing success.

Irrational goal setting is causing serious time delays and unnecessary emotional anxiety worldwide. On the other hand, *continuous learning* in work and life is best practiced while *continuously living.* Continuous improvement doesn't happen without continuous implementation.

What if you could identify the one thing that would help you make all the other things fall into place—thereby skipping over all the needless steps you thought were necessary?

Whether you have it all mapped out or not, whether you love planning or feel suffocated by schedules, it's essential to recognize that those preplanned intentions either happen as planned, happen not as planned, or don't happen at all. Even when your plans are perfectly executed, why not ask yourself if you are doing what you want to be doing in the first place? Is this plan helping you become who you want to become, and is this the best way? And if you get to where you planned on going, was it the place you ultimately wanted to be . . . or just another one of those "stepping-stones" to something else you want?

Leaving an open space for possibility, creativity, and change for something different, spontaneous, or better than you thought should be a default setting on your calendar—if you use one at all.

The dumbest things we do are not getting plans wrong but still following through with wrong plans after we know they aren't in our best interest.

Just because you put a lot of time and effort into something doesn't mean it's the right thing to do—*like knowingly sending a care package to the wrong address.*

Doubling down on bad plans won't deliver your dream. Doubling down on bad plans to preserve your pride is not a recipe for happiness and productivity. Ignorance paired with arrogance (naïveté) is logical, but arrogance paired with awareness (ego) is toxic.

You know better.

To be humble is to be teachable. To be teachable is to be changeable. Your back doesn't have to be up against the wall to experience the fight-or-flight urge when executing . . . A long reckless checklist will do the same thing.

It's not a lesson learned
unless it's a behavior changed.

Meta-Goals, Meta-Decisions, and Metamorphosis

When I work on a new project, I aim, strategize, and operate so that it will provide me more time than I put in—in the immediate to near future. If I aim to have free time five years from now versus five weeks from now, my approach creates a very different mode of operation, but both are largely the same effort.

Imagine the heroic work you do to meet a deadline. Think of how you work differently if you know you can't check in at work for the next week or two. Now imagine if you applied some of that thinking around your future.

No one is more productive than a procrastinator with an impending deadline.

The difference between an operator and an owner is in how they spend their time. You can architect your time differently by organizing what you want in life and still getting the work done. Architects don't build buildings. General contractors sub work out.

Metaphorically, suppose you're legitimately good at digging ditches. In that case, a "strengths test" might tell you you're legitimately good at digging ditches—*so you continue to dig, despite not wanting to or needing to.* Strengths, in this sense, are a time trap. What if you want to stop digging ditches?

You reap what you sow. Seeds become roots become trees. Like a seed, how you spend your time becomes roots that become your life. Plant the seeds of time that you want to enjoy most by doing the things that you want to do most, now. The good news is that time is not a seed—you can leverage time to become virtually any number of things. However, the more you spend your time *not doing that dream,* the *less time you will have in the future to do it*—let alone watch it grow into what you want.

You can humbly approach work to limit the number of tasks impacting your life and time negatively. Courageously create projects that create time, not take time.

CREATE WORK-LIFE FLEXIBILITY PROJECTS

This activity will help you build flexibility as you prioritize your attention with projects built around Personal, Professional, People, and Play Priorities (Four-*Ps*, Final Cause).

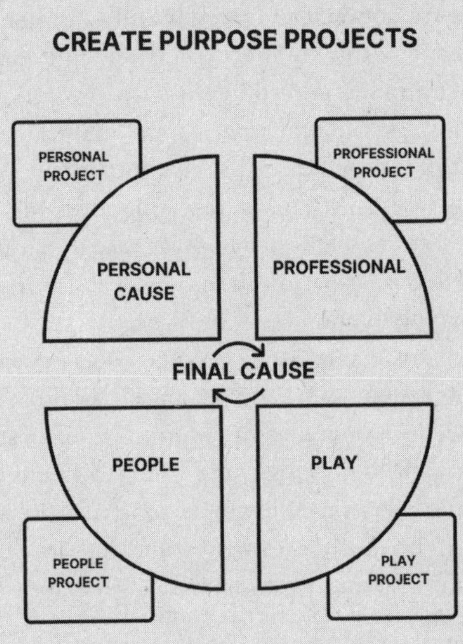

These *Time Tipping Projects* are intended to give you *flexibility*—greater freedom of time to live life productively and happily on your own terms.

In the previous chapter, you identified Final Cause through the Four-*Ps* process. Now you are ready to take each of those *Time Tipped* goals and build projects that drive your freedom and flexibility from the start that can grow into even greater time freedoms and experiences. Showing up in the world in ways that contribute the most and in ways you love most is done in the doing of them, not in the learning. Best practices aren't practiced best in the classroom.

Draw from Your Final Cause Four-*Ps* of Productivity:

1. What is a "project" you can work on for each Final Cause to start making space and time to live your priorities?

   Personal Priority Project:

   Professional Priority Project:

   People Priority Project:

   Play Priority Project:

2. What is the first simple, purposed step you can take today to get this project tipping in the right direction?
3. When do you want to have this project completed (date)?
4. Set daily, weekly, monthly, and annual milestones that will make you realize your goals.

Projects have a beginning and an end. They can fail or succeed. Working on your Purpose Projects moves you from wanting to do something to experimenting and experiencing your dream and instantly becoming a part of that dream—no matter how small.

Think about what has happened so far. We've moved from having an idea to a goal hanging at the end of a timeline to creating a Final Cause environment with a meta-goal and a meta-decision informing your priorities beginning with Purpose Projects. *Time Tipping* nurtures ecosystems so the living of a dream becomes a cultural value, skill, and reality in a fraction of the time.

Purpose Projects: Dreams don't get done until they're due. Projects allow you to pour your learnings into a productive process and help you retain the knowledge learned. Start projects with a deadline today around your future dreams to bring your dreams from the future into the present.

There's a word for moving from transactional time management to transformational *Time Tipping: metamorphosis.*

Download Your Four-Projects Worksheet and Other Anti-Time Management Tools at RichieNorton.com/Time.

BUILD THE CASTLE, THEN THE MOAT.

CHAPTER 3

Build the Castle, Then the Moat

How to Free Up Your Time and Then Protect It

> Love and success, always in that order. It's that simple AND that difficult.
>
> —MISTER ROGERS

Sam Jones started a custom clothing business in 2014 after reading *The Power of Starting Something Stupid* with the dream of having more freedom to travel and spend time with his family and friends. Without knowing it, the business started running him. His relationships and freedom took a backseat as he made himself busy doing things he hated so that "one day" he would have that freedom.

He took steps in the right direction when he started, but when it came down to it, he felt like he had built the wrong type of business because he had no time. He found an opportunity to sell the business and start from scratch again.

Freedom was the goal, not the business.

After selling the business, he reached out to me, and I pointed out that he was too busy building a moat before building the castle. He'd changed the nature of his work but not the order of his priorities.

Sam said:

> I thought the store was my dream. I quickly learned that I was building barriers to my dreams instead. I originally started a business to generate freedom, financial independence, and set my own terms. Without knowing it, I was building walls around myself that kept me from achieving my dreams. I got too occupied worrying about the moat that I never got to the castle. Instead, I needed to build a castle, then build a moat around the castle. Now, as I'm creating new projects, I'm building them around my family, time, and travel. It's such a different mentality, but it's so simple to me now.

Sam elaborated:

> Deep down I found my real goal was to be location independent so that my family could travel where and when we wanted to. You helped me to see that I had to make my values (family, freedom, travel) a priority first, then fit work in the time I had left. I realized I'm doing the same things in two hours that I once thought required eight hours to accomplish. Before, I built my family and freedom around my business. Now, I'm building a business around family and freedom. It's so simple now. Values first, then build the business to support your values.

The castle represents Final Cause—your purpose and priorities. The moat represents work that protects the castle. Free up your time and then protect it. Drop the limiting belief that waiting is just a "part of the process." We've been conditioned to believe that if we "put in our time" and "pay our dues," eventually we will be free to do what we *actually* want to do with our lives.

The ability to freely work and to make money is an incredible privilege. It is a great fortune to have options in how and when and where we work if we can. Not everyone has that comfort. Traditionally, corporations are castles and employees work in the moat. Time management was never designed for the employee to build their own castle. Time management was designed to keep employees digging moats. For example, corporate retirement plans have their roots in employee time management to keep workers for forty years before they leave the workforce—with government tax incentives and penalties to keep it that way. This stick-and-carrot time-management practice becomes less relevant every day.

With the advancement of technology and opportunity, you and I can put our castle—our dreams—first and then build a moat that will help fortify, support, and protect the dream. How we work is a choice, or we must change the order of our priorities if we want more autonomy. Too many people begin with the moat and never get out—even though they could. Start with the castle and then build the moat to free up your time and then protect it.

Collapse Time

In the novel *A Wrinkle in Time*, the magical Mrs. Who and Mrs. Whatsit explain time travel by showing an ant walking across a piece of string. If the ant had to walk from where he was to where he wanted to go, it would be quite a long walk. Mrs. Who brings her hands together, shortening the trip for the ant by bringing the destination to him.

Time Tipping works similarly.

If you know what you want, then the first step is to do the thing that you think is the last step. In so doing, you collapse time and bring the future—your Final Cause—to the now in a tangible way. You can clap timelines together by acting out the finale in the first act.

***Time Tipping* requires you to choose your ideal lifestyle first.** Where do you want to live? How do you want to spend your day? With whom do you want to spend your time? These are the first questions you must ask yourself. Instead of randomly finding work that pays, you prioritize your lifestyle and create or find an income source through entrepreneurship or a career that suits your needs. People generally find a job and live life around it. *Time Tipping* positively turns this work method inside out: live your ideal life and build a job around it.

***Time Tipping* puts your ultimate life choices at the center so you can build your work around it in a supporting, protective role, like a moat around a castle.**

Metaphorically, people may say they want to live in a castle (dream goals), but they begin with the moat (distractions they call "work") and never make it to the castle. Begin with the castle, and then build the moat to create an *impenetrable fortress* for your high priorities.

Time Tippers create Strategic and Economic Moats around their dreams to protect and preserve the dreams so they can pursue ideals without waiting unnecessarily.

When Warren Buffett invests, he looks for companies that have created Economic Moats to protect their economic castle. Buffett wrote, "Both Coke and Gillette have actually increased their world-wide shares of market in recent years. The might of their brand names, the attributes of their products, and the strength of their distribution systems give them an enormous competitive advantage, setting up a protective moat around their economic castles. The average company, in contrast, does battle daily without any such means of protection."

Is your life left unprotected in a daily battle for your time?

Protect your priority time by placing protective moats around it.

Time Tipping: Castle and Moat

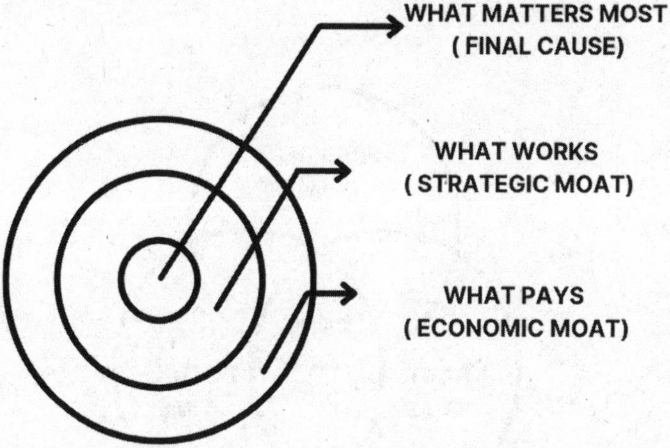

Time Tippers protect their time by intentionally creating *Strategic Moats* (how you work) and *Economic Moats* (how you are paid) to protect your center (Final Cause, purpose, lifestyle, self-expression, values, dreams).

Time freedom is an environment you create so that when things go wrong, you have the flexibility to fix them, prevent recurrences, and restructure for a better future.

Your Perception of the Past and Future Impacts Your Present

Consider the castles and moats you've already created. For a moment, instead of thinking of your life's timeline as past, present, and future, create a space in your mind for how your past caused your present, and how your present has caused your future, and how your vision of the future has caused your present.

The convergence of past, present, and future is where Final Cause lives—the space where you can revolutionize your autonomy, alignment, and available time.

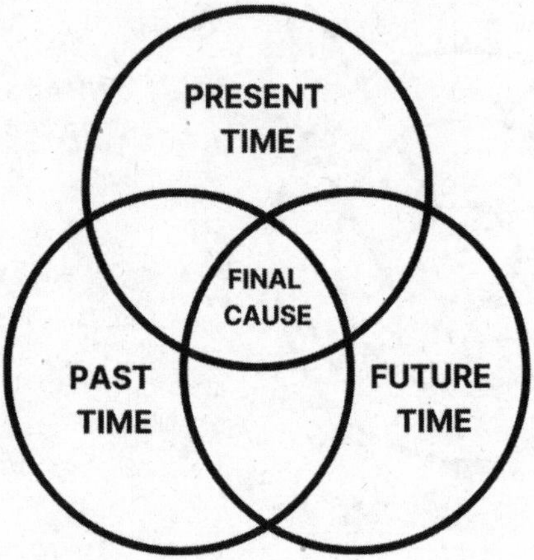

Today you are already living the Final Cause of yesterday (your past). Whatever your experience is now, it was made up by the circumstances and choices of your past (for better or worse). You are currently living in a way that will cause the next version of your life. Why not act in a way that influences the trajectory of your life in the direction you desire? We are all just works in progress. We are constantly changing. You have a say in how your life turns out and how much freedom of time and choice you have (outside of compulsory forces).

Past Time: Think of your life ten years ago. Who were you? Where did you live? How old were you? What were your goals? How much money were you making? What did you do for fun? Who were the most important people in your life? What were you doing for work? What projects were you working on? What was your health like? And so on.

Present Time: If you're like most people, you were a very different person ten years ago. In fact, you may not even feel like you're the same person. You are the same person, of course. However, your experiences, your choices, your life, and the way things unfolded are likely different than you had imagined—for better or for worse. Today, you are probably in a different situation, living under different circumstances. You're building on your past's time, resultant in your present's time, and planning for the future's time. Is today the future you once imagined ten years ago?

Future Time: If your present is different from your past, how effective do you think planning *and waiting* ten years ahead will be? How much more likely would you be to create the future you want in ten years if you began making the essence of those goals happen in the next one to two years? What if you could think and plan and act a little differently—bypassing unnecessary steps that you stacked against yourself thinking they were helping you? If your big-picture dreams in the distant future were possible in one or two years, who's to say they couldn't happen in the next six months, six days, or even right now?

Timing is a decision.

Make room for more time by acknowledging where time got you, what you want to do with your time in the future, and working on it now.

Eliminate, Delegate, and Outsource (EDO)

Rashell Jarvis is in an industry where the hustle mentality is "glorified, 24/7, no sleep, all grind." She unfollowed and removed all of her followers whom she did not know or who did not inspire her and tuned out the noise. She wanted her time back, she didn't want to be distracted, and she wanted a business model that would allow her and her family more freedom and flexibility.

Rashell reached out to me with an extensive menu of ideas she had for her real estate investing clients but wanted to hone in on the products that provided the most value. I told her the best way to know what her clients wanted was simply to ask them. Then I taught her to eliminate, delegate, and outsource everything she *didn't want to do* and *focus on the parts she liked and wanted to do* to get her freedom of time back and organize her work around her priorities.

"I identified what my clients needed," Rashell explained.

> Then I designed my work processes through the EDO method: eliminate, delegate, and outsource. Through the EDO method, I knew I needed to change my current partnership to support the growth and vision of scaling. I started over from zero, but I was on *fire* to make needed changes and knew leading with love, value, and the belief that I deserve this type of success would be built around my family. I have now made a process for my business and applied what my clients said they wanted, and that provides value. I charge more and get paid up front.
>
> I learned that people will pay if the value is there, period. I have now hired talented and skilled people, an accountant, plus an amazing CEO! Currently, my business is operating, and I am not wearing all the hats and every day. I am getting more and more of my time back. My time is used to public speak where I love to be and face-to-face with people teaching how to connect on the human level. Next year looks amazing where we will triple our business and continue to be a force in the real-estate industry nationally! Our family moved from the desert of Arizona to the ocean in Southern California (our dream!) within less than a year of changing our business model because we're living life now!

There is no traditional "selling" when you ask people what they want and give it to them because you're offering them exactly what they want—*they need to know it's available and have the ability to pay.* Identifying both what her ideal clients wanted and what she ideally wanted allowed her to create an ideal new solution that served all parties. It's important to note that Rashell could have created a new business and still been caught in a time trap had she not organized first around the castle she chose for herself.

You can structure your life in such a way that home is at the center and your work protects you and your family. It's the opposite from when your work is at the center of your life and home and family are on the fringe. Your entire life can fall apart at the drop of a downsizing.

Take an Inventory of Your Life

When someone believes their work is meant to enhance their life and others now, how will they invest their time today? Sadly, many people change careers and companies and partnerships only to go back to their time-wasting traditional *busy models.* Instability is the repetition of tactics without a strategy.

Don't echo your past if you want a different future.

Replicating, echoing, and parroting people who don't have the lifestyle you want won't give you the lifestyle you want. I'm not suggesting that your circumstances or priorities are the same as anyone else's. I'm suggesting that you're intentional about whom you follow.

The principle of *Time Tipped flexibility* is that whatever you put in the middle of your life becomes the center of your life from which you operate, wherever you are.

If you want to prioritize service, business, sports, start-ups, investing, education, art, spirituality, fitness, family, travel, giving, play, *whatever*, the principle of *Time Tipped flexibility* cross-pollinates so you can spend more time on each of your choices intentionally.

The castle is where you (want to) live. The moat creates space between you and the unexpected threats to your *priorities' home base* so you can reflect, respond, and get relief.

Your aim in time flexibility is to gain greater influence over the trajectory of your life and make space to dynamically problem-solve.

Every solution creates a problem.

Time Tippers solve for the future problems that inevitably come from future solutions.

This is how you can think differently to create space and time now for an expanding future.

What You've Done So Far

Purposes → Priorities → Projects → Purpose-Driven Mind

You've

- » decided what you think success looks like for you as a Final Cause (Four Purposes).
- » decided what you want to do to spend your time embracing that success (Four Priorities).
- » decided how you will move from distraction to action and live your priorities now (Four Projects).
- » learned the importance of putting your purpose first and creating priorities to protect it, *and not the other way around* (build the castle, then the moat).

Now, let's design the strategy and tactics that will help you decide how to clear the current clutter in your life and work to create space to build your castle—*the place where personal and professional resolve support each other in a virtuous, upward spiral.*

Free Up Your Time with EDO

Eliminate. Delegate. Outsource.

EDO is an anti-time management work-life integration tool to help you design a personalized environment of high trust and high productivity for the daily living of your priorities by thinking through how your work is accomplished now and how it might be done differently to meet your purposes effectually.

As you coordinate with people and leverage existing resources to get things done differently, I caution you not to give yourself a new job that you don't want to do. Replacing one bad job or one bad boss for another bad job or another bad boss doesn't get you anywhere you want. "Begin with the end in mind," as Covey taught, does not mean beginning with the means in mind.

If taken seriously, these two principles will save you a ton of time, money, and headache in creating important work and life projects:

» Begin with ends, not means.

» Delegate results, not methods.

Consider the result, and then architect a way to get there. For example, don't ask others to help you and then micromanage them if you don't want to be a micromanager.

Ends Versus Means. *Time Tippers* thrive in the zone of high impact by discerning between ends and means. Magic happens when you thrive in your zone of high impact and empower others to thrive in their zone of high impact *without mistaking means for ends or beginnings.*

Time Tippers leverage "forcing functions," or "behavior-shaping constraints," to make purpose-aligned decisions now to expand options for a brighter future (building the castle) and create barriers that prevent misaligned decisions (building the moat).

RECLAIM YOUR TIME AND CREATE SPACE WITH EDO

The EDO approach will help you organize your life and reclaim your time.

BUILD THE CASTLE

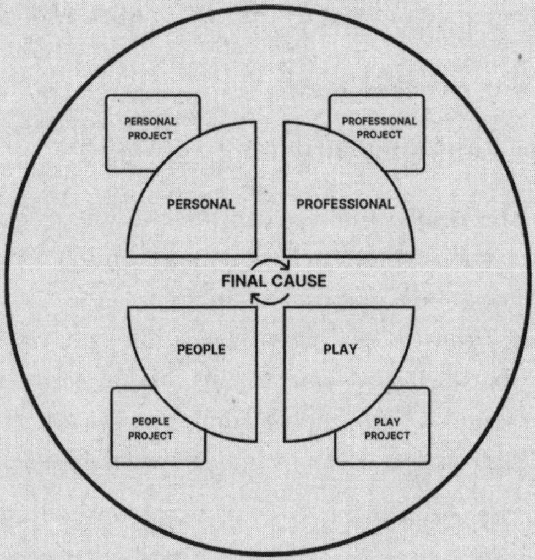

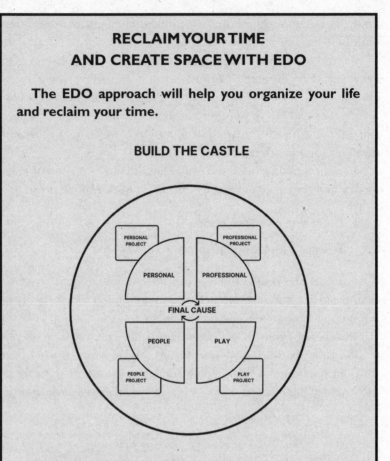

EDO begins by identifying how you currently show up in the world, then identifying how you'd like to show up in the world, and then identifying pathways to get there.

The goal of EDO is to cultivate the seamless living of your various priorities by designing positive forcing functions.

Directions. *Begin with a blank sheet of paper and fold it in half lengthwise. (Or use the prompts here or the worksheet.)*

1. Left side. Write down every single thing you do from the time you wake up to the time you go to bed. You do not have to do this exercise as you go throughout your day. You know the things you do in a day. Jot down everything from taking out the trash to changing kids' diapers to taking the kids to school to working out to hobbies to sports to projects to everything you are responsible for at work and everything you do for fun, and so on. Write down everything you feel like you have to do on average. On one-half sheet of paper, you'll now have your whole life staring back at you in the face. *This is how you are currently showing up in the world.* While our past and our dreams shape our lives, the things we do in the present are how we show up in the present.

Write your daily to-dos here:

____

____

____

____

____

2. Next step. Circle only a few things that you *like and want* to do. Note: You are responsible for many things, but what you like and want to do is what drives you.

3. Right side. Write down the things that you circled on the top right-hand side of the paper that you *like and want* to do. **Write the tasks you're currently doing that you like and want to do:**

____

____

____

____

____

The Life and Work Balance Sheet

What You Like and Want to Do Versus What You Are Doing

4. Take a work-life balance inventory. Consider the left-hand side of the sheet all the things you feel like you, and only you, can accomplish—things you both like and don't like to do. By comparison, the things you like and want to do on the right-hand side are not balanced. Your life is full of things you don't want to do. A cluttered life is a full calendar with the empty promise of free time.

The reason you are asked to identify what you *like and want to do* instead of *what you have to do* or *what you're good at* is subtle but intentional and makes a meaningful difference in your time.

If you didn't feel like you *had* to do something you didn't like or want to do, you'd be less likely to be doing it. Feeling like you must do something can keep you stuck and become too time-consuming if you don't consider another way the task could be accomplished.

What you're good at—your strengths—is important, but just because you're good at something doesn't mean you like and want to do it. While identifying your strengths or taking a personality test can help you perform or understand yourself, they can also stifle your growth when they encourage you to do what you might already know how to do and discourage you from creativity, authenticity, and change.

For example, if a bricklayer is good at laying bricks, don't tell the bricklayer she can't become an architect because her strength is in cement and so is her personality. Traditional time management at its core foundation gets you efficient and faster at bricklaying, not becoming an architect. Instead, if a bricklayer is good at laying bricks but doesn't want to lay bricks, this may or may not have any relevance on her future at all—she can do whatever she wants.

Your past does not define you, but how you think of your future might.

5. Balance your life. Imagine if you were able to find a way to have the things you don't want to do accomplished without having to do them yourself while maintaining integrity and quality in their completion. As a brain exercise, if everything you didn't want to do but felt like you had to do were done without you doing it yourself, what would happen? Theoretically, if everything you don't want to do is handled, then everything you want to do on the left-hand side of the sheet would match everything you're doing on the right-hand side of the sheet. In this sense, your life is balanced.

This thought process may sound far-fetched, but it's not. While it may not all happen at once, learning to think and act differently is a learned skill set. What would it take to make it happen?

Anything you can eliminate, delegate, or outsource gives you your time back.

Using the Pareto Principle, does your day roughly look like it is made up of ***20 percent of what you like and want*** *and* ***80 percent of what you don't like and want***? If so, then through an aligned, thoughtful process of ***eliminating, delegating, and outsourcing what you don't want to do***, you would theoretically **get back 80 percent of your time** (plus the mental bandwidth associated with it).

This is Time Tipping.

6. Unbalance your life in the direction you want to go. How would you feel if you had 80 percent of your time available and the other 20 percent spent on what you like and want to do? Would you leave the 80 percent of time open, fill it by doubling down on the 20 percent you want and like doing, or fill it with new ideas, projects, and dreams?

While this concept of actively freeing up your time may sound foreign—and of course every situation is different with various grades of adaptability—this is the process *Time Tippers* use to clear the clutter and make time to work on their professional and personal dreams.

Now it's your turn.

Group your tasks.

7. Eliminate.

Look back at the list on the left-hand side and ask yourself, **"Which of these things could I cross out and eliminate?"** And put an *E* for "eliminate" next to them. Ask yourself, **"If I cross it off, would it matter?" If it won't impact anyone negatively, eliminate it from your to-do list.** There might not be that many, but there's more than you realize. Cross them off your list.

Write down what you're eliminating:

____

____

____

____

____

8. Delegate.

Then look through the list again and ask yourself, **"Which ones can I delegate?"** And put a *D* for "delegate" next to them. You don't need to know to whom or how you are delegating right now. You're just grouping tasks that you want to eventually delegate. **Delegation, in this sense, does not mean you're paying anyone to do these tasks.** Delegation could be reassigning, realigning, or switching roles at work or home. Is there someone who likes and wants to do this task?

Write down what you're delegating:

____

____

____

____

____

9. Outsource.

Look at your list and think, **"Which things can I outsource?"** And put an *O* for "outsource" next to them. **This would mean you would pay somebody else to do the task.** Maybe you don't want to mow your own lawn, or you take your dress clothes to the dry cleaner, or you hire a CPA, or pay someone to build a website, or partner with someone on a project, and so forth.

Write down what you're outsourcing:

____

____

____

____

____

Hypothetically, suppose you were to eliminate, delegate, and outsource everything on the left side of the paper except the things you like and want to do. In that case, suddenly both sides of the page are perfectly balanced between what you need and what you want to do. They say it builds character to do things you don't want to do—*this is one of those things*. Sometimes the most challenging things you do are the things you want. Put priorities first.

This is your life's balance sheet. Balance, on paper, looks better than being unbalanced in the wrong direction. You can look at your sheet and imagine unbalancing your life with forward motion in the direction you want to go. "Oh, now I have 80 percent more time. What am I going to do with it?"

How to use EDO. The purpose of EDO is to organize your life with priorities. When a new job, task, or project comes into your life, you can ask yourself if you like and want to do it. If so, does it bring you closer to living your Four-*Ps* or further away? Then, if you want or need to pursue it, ask if it's something you will do or if it should be eliminated, delegated, or outsourced.

The castle is built upon the things you like and want to do that serve your purposes and interests. The moat around your castle is dug through the power of EDO.

When the EDO thought process becomes an active reality in your life, everything changes. If you've ever wondered how to organize your tasks and free up tons of time, now you know.

Operationalizing your decision-making process based on protecting your "castle" will reclaim your time, change the way you work, and enhance your quality of life.

Imagine if you spent your days doing only what you like and want to do, while everything that needed to get done still got done, with loads of available time to do whatever you want.

You can architect a future that looks different from the present if you want. Life is going to change moving forward regardless of intent. You might as well build from the metaphorical castle you'd like to live in.

What would life be like if you created space to be inventive, innovative, and do new projects that you like and want to do? You can start building your castle upon the works that you like and want to do that serve your best interests. Building the castle first gives you purpose and flexibility.

E.D.O.

ELIMINATE | **D**ELEGATE | **O**UTSOURCE

EVERYTHING I DO IN A DAY	EVERYTHING I WANT TO DO

PART II
PRACTICES

Move from Distraction to Action

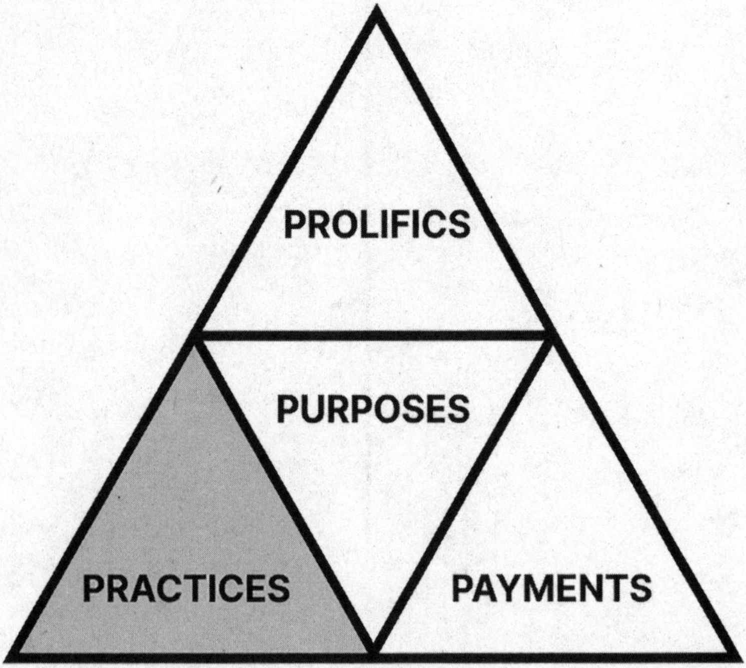

MOVE FROM DISTRACTION TO ACTION.

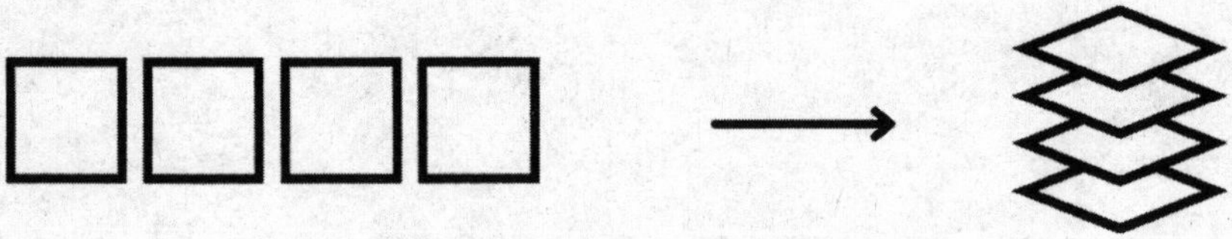

PROJECT STACKING

CHAPTER 4

Stack Your Projects—Project Stacking

How to Make Time Work for You

> Consider thyself to be dead, and to have completed thy life up to the present time; and live according to nature the remainder which is allowed thee.
>
> —MARCUS AURELIUS,
> Roman emperor and Stoic philosopher

As an immigrant to America, Ben Willson came with the dream of freedom. He became an entrepreneur, and as each business grew, so did his responsibilities—working eighteen-hour days.

He said, "At first it didn't feel like work, but very quickly that faded. With more clients came more problems, and I became overwhelmed. I slid down the slide of depression into the darkest moments of my life. I no longer wanted to be in business. I wanted someone to fire me from the job I had built for myself. I let the business slowly burn away."

Ben learned about the joy of *Time Tipping* and broke the patterns he had developed early in his life. Ben said, "I wanted to be happy. I wanted to wake up feeling like I was helping others in their businesses and be a champion for entrepreneurship. I learned how to rethink how I spend my time building a business. I learned how to spot what would move the needle and how to avoid time-sucking activities. As my mindset shifted, so did my happiness. I now have time to work out, journal, play with my dog, go for long walks, and spend quality time with my wife."

He learned the power of *Project Stacking*—merging his various Purpose Projects so an act in one area can create an array of many desired results in other areas of work and life.

Ben explained, "I no longer work eighteen hours a day. I now work six to seven hours a day maximum, and yet my results are five to ten times more. I have time to think through my problems, and I have a clear path of what I want to accomplish in my life. Typically, I would have thought I would have to wait ten years to fulfill my dreams."

Operationalize Your *Time Tipped* Lifestyle

Time Tippers leverage a powerful combination of what I call *Project Stacking*, *Work Syncing*, and *Expert Sourcing* to create an autonomy in work and life.

1. Project Stacking
2. Work Syncing
3. Expert Sourcing

Practicing these three principles can *expand* and *protect* your available time as a Strategic Moat around Final Cause.

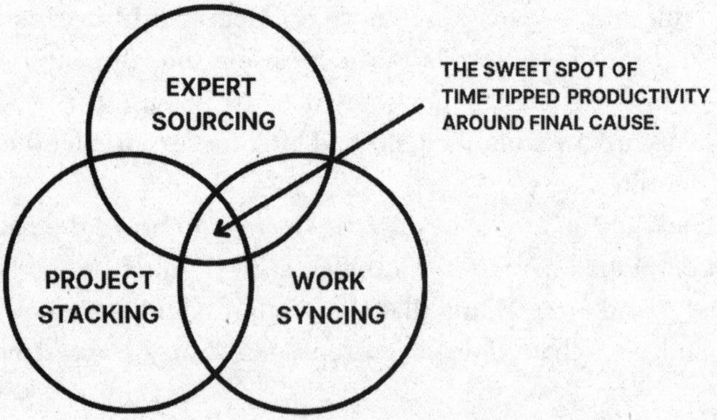

Project Stacking, Work Syncing, and Expert Sourcing operationalize the way you work to make freedom of time not only a habit (a Strategic Moat) but a sustainable habitat (the castle).

Create a Strategic Moat Around Your Ideal Way of Life

How do two people with basically the same job lead such different personal lives? They do so in three ways:

» *Priorities*—Good things happen by prioritizing your attention, not by managing time.

» *Practices*—Dreams become nightmares when we turn goals into jobs.

» *Payments*—How you're paid determines autonomy. The job of a dream is to set you free.

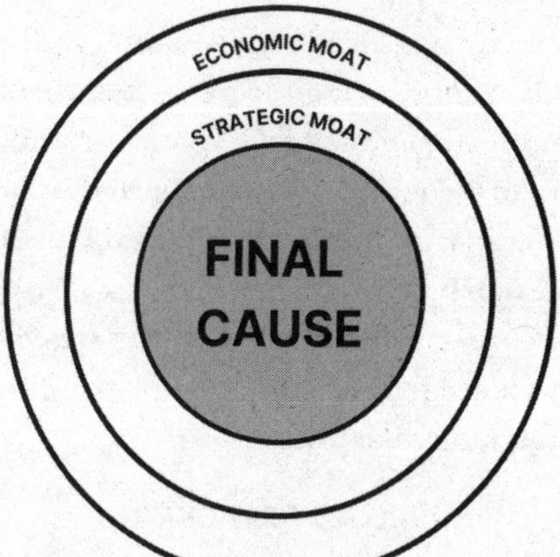

Define Your *Time Tipping* Project Terms

Projects live for a deadline. Deadlines are critical to projects, but too often project managers will stagger, silo, and structure project timelines without considering shared resources or *cross-project pollination.*

Project management **is notorious for executing on a strategy without considering strategic intent or the consequences of implementation**

related to the desired result. Traditional time and project management will often, *sometimes intentionally*, make the fulfillment of an overarching blueprint take years when it could have possibly taken months—or, worse, it didn't need to have been done at all. A never-ending job is "job security."

» ***Project Stacking*** (along with Work Syncing and Expert Sourcing) enables you to complete multiple projects at the same time with proper *priority blending* and *project overlap.*

» ***Priority Blending*** is the art of discovering and designing priorities so multiple high-value outcomes can happen under one aligned activity.

» ***Project Overlap*** is the art of discovering and designing the internal networks of two or more projects to perform one aligned activity without the cost in time and money of redundant resources.

The key to increasing productivity, autonomy, and freedom of time is to use your energy as a giver to be creative in helping others instead of overprotecting your ego. Be resourceful. It sounds basic, but it's important to recognize that ***your humanity is your strength***. Lean into your creative capacity, not your perceived limitation. Blend your priorities and overlap projects to save time, create opportunities, and tap into robust ecosystems that increase your ***availability***, ***ability***, and ***autonomy*** to serve more people.

Project Stacking looks like this:

PROJECT STACKING

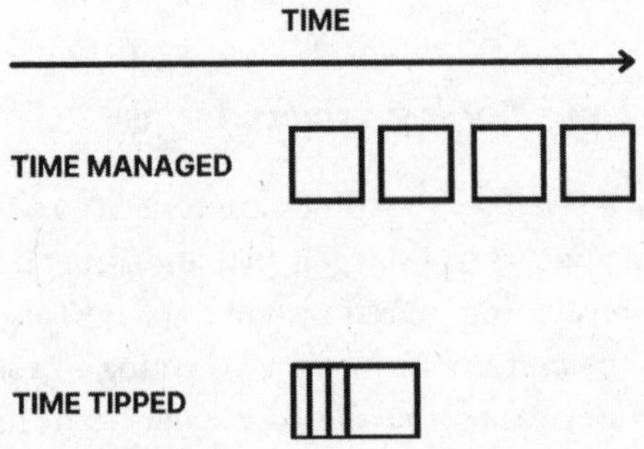

Like tipping over one domino that completes the rest, Project Stacking is a seamless act to make the doing of one good thing happily accomplish many great things.

This is the transformational question that I asked myself when I was twenty-one that got me stacking my future dream projects into my daily living (despite lack of time, money, and resources):

"How can I make money and meaning without waiting years to do so?"

This question helped me take the projects I was working on and find ways to incorporate them with my future dreams and find mentors and resources to help me overcome my lack of experience. These Project Stacks, of course, then created a new work environment and culture around my big-picture dreams where I could experiment, get experience, and generate results that would have otherwise taken years or decades.

Take a Mindful Approach, Not Mindless Action

Project Stacking uses both linear and lateral thinking to generate the compounding effect of *concentric circles of time.* One meta-decision makes an impact at the center of your life and generates circles of time-expanding waves—like throwing a rock in a pond.

Commitment to traditional time management's linear thinking can become disorienting to the point of making you lose opportunities of peripheral vision to the threat of tunnel vision.

Making Project Stacked decisions and taking a mindful approach to achievement moves you from distraction to action by making your priorities front and center, not background noise.

> "Don't make a hundred decisions
> when one will do."
>
> —JIM COLLINS, bestselling author of *Good to Great*, who said he learned this lesson from Peter Drucker, the legendary management consultant

Collins explains:

> In Drucker's view, we rarely face truly unique, one-off decisions. And there is an overhead cost to any good decision: it requires argument and debate, time for reflection and concentration, and energy expended to ensure superb execution. So, given this overhead cost, it's far better to zoom out and make a few big generic decisions that can apply to a large number of specific situations, to find a pattern within—in short, to go from chaos to concept. Think of it as akin to Warren Buffett making investment decisions. Buffett learned to ignore the vast majority of possibilities almost as background noise. Instead, he made a few big decisions—such as the decision to shift from buying mediocre companies at very cheap prices to buying great earnings machines at good prices—and then replicated that generic decision over and over again. For Drucker, those who grasp Buffett's point that "inactivity can be very intelligent behavior" are much more effective than those who make hundreds of decisions with no coherent concept.

Stack projects so one decision does the job of a thousand across multiple priorities.

Ultimately, it is possible to blend your life's priorities instead of keeping them siloed off from one another. Project Stacking views goal prioritization holistically. Waiting for one thing to happen before the next is status quo linear thinking, time-consuming, and often unnecessary.

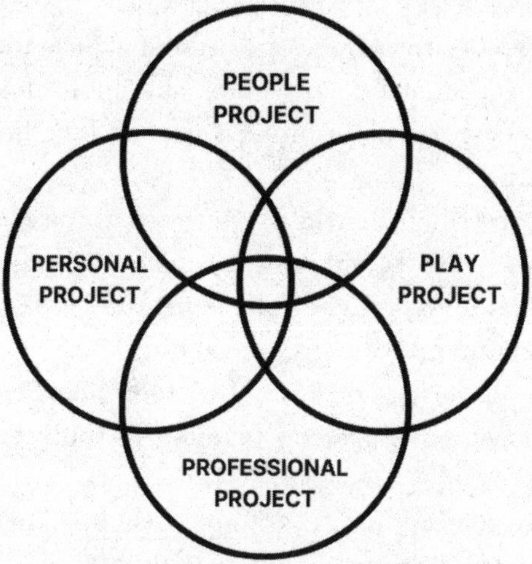

PRIORITY PROJECT STACKING

Don't Multitask, Project Stack

Project Stacking is not multitasking.

» Project Stacking can help you do one thing that accomplishes many things.

» Project Stacking can end the pain of living an unlived life inside of you.

» Project Stacking integrates your work and life to help you accomplish your ideals without compromise.

» Project Stacking can accomplish many high-value goals at work while facilitating an abundance of high-value available time at home (or anywhere).

» Project Stacking can help you start, scale, and streamline projects.

Project Stacking creates an interlocked network—multitasking does not.

Elon Musk's three companies, Tesla, SpaceX, and SolarCity, are public examples of Project Stacking. At first glance, these enterprises appear to be distinct and unrelated, but upon closer inspection, it's clear that these are three projects stacked together and working interdependently.

It's been described that Musk "sees the three companies as an interconnected network, and wants to make sure that each leg of the tripod can help out the others." The companies cross-pollinate, sharing technology and growing his overarching vision.

But you don't have to be Elon Musk to Project Stack.

Project Stacking fits projects together to fulfill the mission of a bigger picture.

This is possible because there are harmonies between projects through *purpose fit.* The success of one fuels the success of the others. However, the failure of one project does not collapse the others because they are interdependent, not dependent, on one another.

***Project symbiosis* makes it more effectual to have three projects stacked than just one alone, and it and saves time—the sum is greater than the parts.**

Done correctly, Project Stacking will help you live your highest priorities without wasting time on lower-priority tasks but still get the necessary tasks done responsibly as you eliminate, delegate, or outsource. By so doing, you will have freed up your time to do only what you want to do—increasing your available time to do what you want (or do nothing at all).

What will you do with your newly found freedom of time? For ambitious people, their goals become all-consuming. You'll have the time to explore your new ideas, help others, spend time with your family, travel, be more productive on your current work, or create new projects.

The freedom of more choices presents a new problem—when you have an abundance of options, what *do you* do? Whatever you do, it's a choice, and you've created an environment where you can make those choices without failing on your high-priority commitments.

Create an Interlocking Support System

Keira Poulsen had a massive breakdown. Old trauma memories surfaced that led her to feeling suicidal and broken.

Keira said, "But, in that moment of choosing to live or not, I chose life. I chose to live fully and to do everything I was inspired to do. I later started a publishing house for women, but found I had grown it so fast and didn't know how to navigate life as a mother to five kids and running a business. My business was slowly taking over my life. And my income began to decrease as my exhaustion level started to take over." It was at this point that Keira decided to change the way she was operating her business.

She said, "I use the principle to build my business around my family, not the other way around." She created a positive constraint to end work by four so she could be with her kids after school. She also changed her offers and pricing to reflect valuing her time and the value she was providing. Keira leveraged Project Stacking to interlock her family priorities with her business priorities and her personal-time priorities. She effectively created a *project tripod* of time optimization that kept her life stable and her view in focus.

Keira said, "Immediately, my monthly revenue went from $3,000 to $11,000. Family life was doing better, and my work seemed to mirror that in all the ways. Only nine months later, I hit my first $70,000 month, which turned out to be my easiest sales month yet. This principle has proven to be true, time and time again." The constraints that Keira created to respect her time with family, clients, and personally allowed her to free up space in her mind to come up with creative solutions that helped her live today bigger than her imagined future.

Through the lens of a *Time Tipped* mindset, your priorities can overlap as an interlocking support system (*not a series of trade-offs isolated from one another*) to generate both money and meaning through Project Stacking.

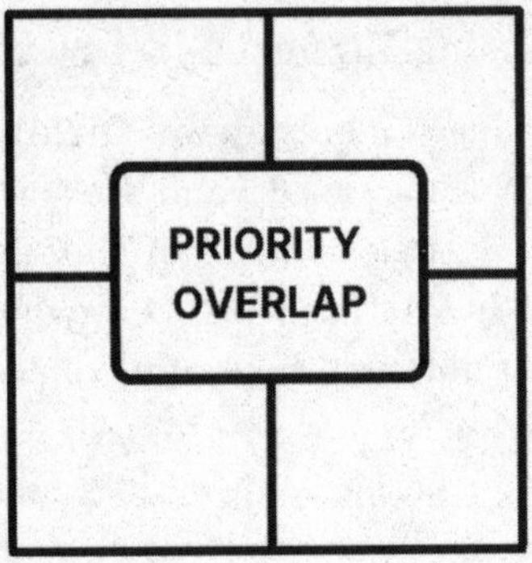

Project Stacking Is an Extension of Your Thinking

Steve Jobs used projects as an extension of his wide array of ideas. "Although widely recognized as a marketing and technology guru," reports the Darton Group, "Jobs . . . was largely successful because of his project-based thought process for running his business and bringing products to market. As a matter of fact, he may be the most transcendent business change agent in terms of an approach to executing projects that ultimately changed not just the business world, but the world we live in." Project Stacking stacks the odds of success in the favor of the project stacker.

If you want to get going on an idea, start projects. But if you want to "put a dent in the universe," stack projects. Project Stacking is a *success accelerator.*

Here are three ways Project Stacking can help you save time now and create time in the future while living from Final Cause.

Project Stacking Accomplishes Many Tasks at the Same Time

When Project Stacking is executed correctly, bold fundamental shifts at work become a catalyst for solving work-life integration problems, reaching many goals simultaneously, and *Tipping Time.* Project Stacking is not to be confused with multitasking. Project Stacking is the art of creating projects that multitask for you, so you don't have to. Multitasking is largely a split-focus, personal, multioperational role that can end focus and slow things down. Project Stacking unites resources around a common cause and generates multifaceted results without distraction—accelerating the fulfillment of goals and enhancing focus.

Project Stacking Is Executing Where Purpose Overlaps

For example, imagine if my Four Priorities and their projects are to be healthy, spend more time with my spouse, earn an extra $1,000 a month, and volunteer to serve others. I might ask myself questions like these:

» How can I go about making these desires overlap?

» Is it possible that I could do something fun that could combine all four?

» What if I took my family on a trip that involved hiking, spending time together, and doing a service project, and this encouraged me to find a way to make more money to fund it?

» What if there were a way to make money indirectly so that I could live this way as often as I liked?

» What if there were a way to make money from this project directly?

» What if another organization already does this such that we could *mission match*—making our mission match with theirs by collaborating?

The creative thought process that can come from mixing projects and sharing resources to save time and make meaning is practical and profitable. One question, one conversation, one idea can change things dramatically.

Time Tippers Avoid Transactional Solutions and Look to Create Transformational Solutions— That Also Solve Future Problems

Every solution creates a problem. When you're Project Stacking, you're also looking beyond the potential collaborations to the after-effect challenges they may create. You don't want to work your way out of one box only to box yourself into another.

Time Tippers look toward where they are going and use Project Stacking to solve the future problems that present-day solutions create. Project Stacking saves time day after day, week after week, year after year by avoiding problems that shouldn't exist in the first place.

When you Project Stack with time intent, you overcome outdated, routine, time-consuming modi operandi for strategic, aligned, time-creating autonomy.

The more priority overlap you can create, the more one decision has an impact on all of your various dreams, priorities, goals, and ways of living.

Dreams Don't Get Done Until They're Due

Your next big Final Cause projects may not feel urgent right now because they're not screaming for attention—*unless there is an impending deadline.* Use deadlines to your advantage, especially if you're a procrastinator, precrastinator, or perfectionist. The pain of big-picture dreams degrading into regrets is demoralizing. You're one decision away from turning future regret into today's imperative.

In this case, Project Stacking can help you better show up for your new reality by reducing the tendency to *procrastinate, precrastinate, and perfectionate.*

When your life's work revolves around your life's dreams, you'll feel more productive and have more autonomy and flexibility. *It's relaxing.* Ironically, you may feel like a *procrastinator* when you're aware of how efficiently you're using your time and how much more you could be doing with your free time. You may also fall into the temptation to waste time fussing around by *precrastinating* or avoiding your most important roles and goals and blaming it on *perfectionism.*

» Procrastination is impulsiveness.

» Precrastination is anxiousness.

» Perfectionism is avoidance.

Procrastination. Don't be impulsive on low-priority tasks to avoid high-priority living—like filling up on bread at dinner instead of the main course. Instead, use procrastination to your advantage. **Remember: No one is more productive than a procrastinator with an impending deadline.**

Precrastination. Don't appear to be productive for the sake of looking productive. **When you do the stuff that doesn't matter, you have no time to do the stuff that does.** Ironically, when you do the stuff that does matter first, you somehow have time to do all that you want to do anyway—a refreshing waterfall effect of productivity.

Perfectionism. Oftentimes people blame perfectionism as the cause of procrastination. However, perfectionism serves a different purpose. Perfectionists want to make things perfect. **To that end, perfectionists will choose activities that are low risk that they can do well right now instead of working on big projects because they will require more time and attention to do them right—saving them for later.**

Perfectionists fall into a trap of doing less important, easier things that they can do well now instead of living out their dreams because they can't be done perfectly. However, nothing is perfect because perfection is always under construction—this makes perfectionism all the more time-draining.

Yet *imperfectionists* can make more "perfect" things than perfectionists because they have more opportunities to try. Perfection is born of imperfection. **In *Project Stacking*, be attentive to proliferation to create perfection, not polishing a silhouette.**

Prepare, Don't Overprepare

Overpreparedness is the downfall of the well intentioned. Overpreparedness has stopped people their whole lives from doing what they want to do.

Why do people with lesser experience keep doing what you wish you could?

One of the reasons the overprepared fail is because they are afraid of ambiguity in search of certainty. However, the most certain things in life are prisons of our own making. When you look at your most important priorities, live like overpreparedness has stopped you your whole life from doing what you want to do—*and you'll start doing.*

The opposite of certainty in life is called freedom. If you want to be free, you must be willing to advance your life into the uncertain.

- ***Effective.*** Drop the act that you know exactly what you're doing, and you'll know what to do.
- ***Efficient.*** Use a beginner's mind, embrace continuous learning, and make the next phase of your life your best life.
- ***Effectual.*** Be strategic in *time intent* by thinking of your desired future, bringing its essence into your presence now, and acting from that energy moving forward.

The relationship between Final Cause and *final effect* is effectuality.

Project Stacking is the critical domino in making everything else you do (and want to do) fall into place. Likewise, think of all the open space behind that first domino—the space where nothing falls down because nothing is there. Keep that space open and clean and available to hold space for meaningful spontaneity and possibility.

Life is too short and too fragile to close yourself off to something amazing you didn't already have in mind.

Effectualism. Integrating your priority projects as a suite is effective, efficient, and effectual—and it also sets you up for greater testing, practicing and proving your ideas. The beauty of a project in the first place is that you don't have to commit to forever, and it has a beginning and an end.

In Project Stacking, you get to taste your future before having "made it." As you begin to live your ideals in the present, you may like it and double down. Or you may learn the dream wasn't all it was cracked up to be and not something you actually enjoy—*saving you possibly decades of categorically working toward the wrong thing.*

All of your priorities being lived in harmony simultaneously isn't an illusion—it's what happens when you erase prefabricated timing.

No more waiting. If you keep overcomplicating your dreams, you'll never learn how wonderful it feels to step into them. You've arrived. Take a deep breath, and simply experiment with what's right in front of you by starting projects and stacking them. Integrating personal and professional joy instead of keeping them isolated is an organic, natural way of life—a lifestyle that organizational time management has kept you from.

Stack Projects Like the Rock—Like Legos—Like a Brand

Perhaps one of the most prominent displays of Project Stacking comes from Dwayne "The Rock" Johnson. He's become one of the highest-paid actors of all time, but he doesn't stop there. He has several companies built around his interests and opportunities to help others. It would be hard to find a post he shares that doesn't include many of his projects being promoted or merged or somehow connected all simultaneously. He ties it all together under one umbrella with his meta-value.

Who would think a Disney movie, tequila, a sportswear brand, an energy drink, training shoes, an upcoming movie, a production studio, a television series, working out, and spending time with your family in Hawaii would all be related? They aren't, but by way of the connector—The Rock—his projects are an extension of his lifestyle and can seamlessly be joined, promoted, or stacked together like Legos.

Stack Time

Stop thinking small. Think of a project you're working on now:

- How could you stack a project to make it twice, three times, or a hundred times or more as productive?
- How can you overlap and unite projects to a common cause?
- How can you do something now in a way that will create loads more time later?

Your goal as a *Time Tipper* is to set things in motion, not do everything yourself.

STACK YOUR PROJECTS

Project Stacking helps you create a moat around your time by combining resources.

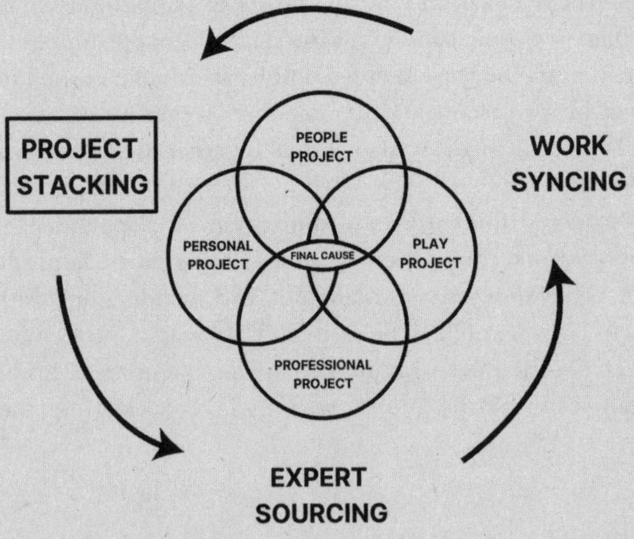

Project Stacking can help you have work-life flexibility and live out your Final Cause in the here and now, instead of years from now. If you do the work, *really do it*, you'll find solutions, but you'll also uncover a maze of problems that may have been created over years of doing work linearly.

Change the way you work by creating Project Stacks:

1. Project Stack: Look at your Four Final Cause Projects.

2. Declutter current time: To accomplish these goals, decide what tasks can be combined to reduce wasted time by reducing the number of steps it takes to achieve them.

You're looking for tasks that may have been done in isolation that you can bring together so that a single effort helps you accomplish many goals at the same time—like compound interest but applied to work effort.

3. Declutter future time: Now look and see and think from inside your Four-*Ps Final Cause Projects*. Where is their task overlap? What efforts can you combine?

4. Stack your *Final Cause Projects*: Do the Castle-Moat activity from Chapter 3 for each of your Four Projects.

5. Stacked! Look at what you've just done! If you did this activity correctly, you've been able to reduce the number of steps it takes to accomplish your goals, and you've decided on what you can do right now. You've laid the foundation for your metaphorical castle, and you've begun building a strategic and tactical moat around your dreams by eliminating, delegating, and outsourcing the parts that you don't want to do so you can focus on what you do best, flexibly.

You've combined your tasks in a way that one choice can intentionally, positively impact many Final Cause outcomes.

WORK SYNCING

CHAPTER 5

Sync Your Work—Work Syncing

How to Sync Your Work with Your Life

> You have to look at a total life, not just your professional life, your personal life. It's a total life and all of the pieces have to snap to grid.
>
> —AICHA EVANS, CEO of Zoox and head of Amazon Automation

Their two-seater prop plane ran out of gas in a remote area over northern Arizona. The sun had set, and the light grew dimmer by the minute.

It was the 1940s, and my grandma and grandpa piloted a joyride. They loved flying together as a young couple. Only, this flight had a problem. The gas leaked, and they had nowhere to land.

It was too dark to land safely—even if they could find a field between the pines.

They noticed a one-off restaurant in the distance.

They had an idea.

What if they radioed and asked the customers to line their cars along the tiny dirt road with their headlights on so they could land? And that's precisely what happened.

I think it's safe to say that I wouldn't be here had they not been so fortunate and resourceful.

Synchronization Requires Resourcefulness

Sometimes we forget how resourceful we can be until there is an emergency.

Resourcefulness in concert with our priorities is so underrated in our everyday lives that we often leave ourselves circling and running out of gas when we could be coordinating a way to land in time for dinner safely.

Work Syncing looks like this:

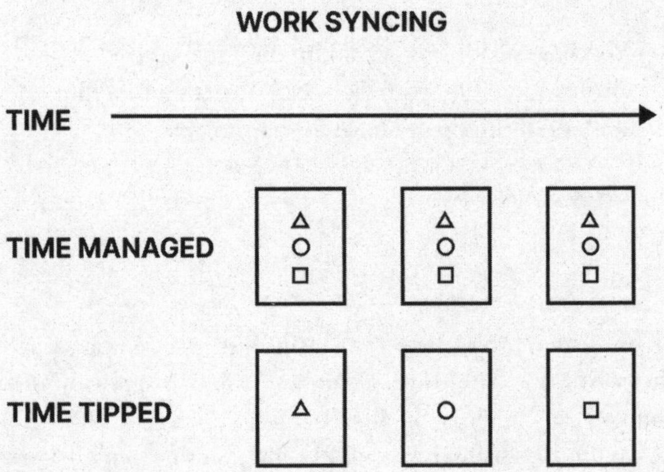

Synchronize Your Work with Your Life

Have you ever worked all day and felt like you got nothing done?

***Work Syncing* helps you be highly productive by (a) syncing your attention (b) with your priorities (c) when it's most timely.**

Even if resources are abundant, how and when you use tools and creativity to achieve your aim is what makes the difference between producing or not.

Purpose versus purposeful. A tiny dirt road, a radio in a restaurant, and customers with cars are not resources *purposed* to landing a plane in the dark. However, these resources became *purposeful* when my grandma and grandpa gave them meaning and unified them to a common cause.

Purpose is not purposeful without synchronizing meaning to an aspiration.

Purposefully leading your life means more than living with positive intent.

» A purposefully lived day shows up as *mission congruence* across *thought, behavior, and direction.*

» Work Syncing requires *awareness, attention, and alignment.*

» Work Syncing looks like creatively combining purposeful resources to accomplish your priority projects.

Sometimes purposeful resources are obvious, but often they may seem unrelated, requiring you to create space for new ideas with open-mindedness for *project innovation.*

What's the purpose of your dream?

Work Syncing embeds purpose into the culture of your dream from the start as a conscious decision to make your dream and its process fit to purpose.

Create Space to Work Sync

Is there anything that you carry around that is a resource but is unused and holding you back from moving forward?

Unloading what is holding you back is neither an art nor a science—*it's a decision.* You can create space by unlearning what you learned, relearn what you learned, or learn something new. You can create space by acting from Final Cause. Whether you subscribe to minimalism or maximalism in your life and business, *you decide what fulfills your purpose.*

Work Syncing is getting to the space you most want to create (mentally, physically, emotionally, economically, socially, and so on) standing right where you are, right now—*and thus creating the essence of your dream from start time.* Acting from Final Cause creates both breadth and depth in Work Syncing and meaning making.

When in doubt about where to sync your time, err on the side of generosity.

How to Sync Attention, Priorities, and Time

The first airplane to cross the United States took forty-nine days—nineteen days off schedule.

Airplanes had been around for only about eight years when publishing magnate William Hearst announced the Hearst prize in October 1910. The award was $50,000 (more than $1 million in today's money) to the first aviator to fly coast-to-coast, in either direction, in thirty days by the deadline, November 1911—a year's time.

Cal Rodgers decided the adventure was worth his time, but this project had two problems: he didn't have a plane, and he didn't know how to fly.

Consider the collaborative way Rodgers synced his attention to his aspirations by uniting ideas, people, and resources to accomplish his Final Cause.

1. ***No tools.*** There were no gauges or instruments or airport traffic-control towers to guide him along the way.

2. ***No know-how.*** Cal Rodgers didn't know how to fly, so he learned—only months before the competition's deadline.

    > "Rodgers spent 90 minutes with Orville Wright receiving instruction in June 1911. That was it for the entirety of his training as a pilot."

3. ***No airplane.*** He didn't have an airplane, so he entered and won a competition to buy one—becoming the first private citizen to buy an airplane from the Wright brothers.

> "In August 1911, he took off as a soloist as part of an air endurance contest and won the $11,000 prize. That money allowed him to purchase a Wright Model B airplane that was modified as the Model EX."

4. ***No money.*** He needed more money for his transcontinental flight, so he got a sponsor and named the *Vin Fiz* airplane after the new Vin Fiz grape soda.

> "Rodgers found a sponsor in J. Ogden Armour. The meatpacking tycoon wanted to promote a new grape soda drink, and with the sponsorship, the first aerial billboard was born . . ."

5. ***No team.*** He needed a team on the ground, and so he used the grape soda funds to hire them.

> "The trip would require numerous spare parts including wings and major fuselage sections, as well as a crew of mechanics and support staff that ended up filling a three-car train."

6. ***Failure.*** On September 17, 1911, Cal Rodgers began his journey from New York to California—he crashed the next day.

> On September 17, 41 days after he had obtained his pilot's certificate, Cal Rodgers had the *Vin Fiz* assembled on the Sheepshead Bay racetrack near Long Island, New York. A large crowd had gathered. Most of them doubted the trip could be made.
>
> Rodgers managed to make it more than 100 miles, landing in a field in Middletown, New York. The next morning, in what would become the first of many accidents along the way, the *Vin Fiz* snagged a tree on takeoff, and both pilot and airplane suffered damage. After a few

> days of repairs on the wing, the fuselage and Rodgers' head, the *Vin Fiz* continued, eventually making it to Chicago three weeks later.

7. ***Purpose.*** There was no way Cal Rodgers would meet the thirty-day coast-to-coast goal, but the goal wasn't his purpose. In fact, he'd brought crutches along with him in anticipation of the challenges he'd face—*Time Tipping has its ups and downs.*

    > With the 30-day deadline looming, it was apparent there would be no prize. But Rodgers wanted to complete the trip and continued with his entourage of mechanics and supporters. The aircraft would end up making more than 70 stops before landing at the designated goal in Pasadena, California, on Nov. 5.
    >
    > Rodgers made more than 15 crash landings and numerous hospital visits during the trip. The plane had been repaired and rebuilt so many times during the trip that . . . little of the original aircraft made it to California. Rodgers suffered numerous injuries during the flight: a broken leg in Arizona, shrapnel in his arm from a blown cylinder, and too many cuts, scrapes and bruises to count.

8. ***Final Cause.*** The money incentive of the contest and the deadline got him started, but *Final Cause* and *Work Syncing* won him the fulfillment of achieving his dream—a dream that was lived out all the way along—from sea to shining sea.

In fact, when Rodgers was crashing into a chicken yard or trying to avoid souvenir seekers from dismantling his aircraft or chasing away cows in a field or trying to land when there was no light or pushing the plane for miles through the desert or having doctors remove steel splinters from his body—Cal Rodgers spread joy because he was living joyfully.

"It was becoming obvious that Cal would never make it to the Pacific by the deadline. Cal did not admit defeat, but continued on, arriving in Chicago on October 8. To celebrate, Cal put on an aerobatic show for the prisoners in Joliet Prison. By the time he reached Marshall, Missouri, he had covered 1,398 miles, breaking the existing world record for cross-country airplane flying. Again, he staged an exhibit of aerobatics to celebrate."

When Cal Rodgers landed, a Pasadena newspaper reported him saying, "I don't feel much tired. The trip was not a hard one, all things considered. Indeed, I believe that in a short time, we will see it done in 30 days and perhaps less. I was never worried at any stage of the game, not even when it looked as if it was all off. I knew I'd get through even if only to show up the fellows who laughed at me."

A 456-hour time delay on an airplane today might feel frustrating to you, but it led to airplanes making that same crossing now in a mere matter of hours. Cal Rodgers said, "I expect to see the time when we shall be carrying passengers in flying machines from New York to the Pacific Coast in three days."

That's synced purpose.

Time is relative.
Meaning is subjective.
Living purposefully is a choice.

Attention to aspirations is good, but syncing your thoughts and behaviors with your direction fulfills Final Cause with worthwhile work and meaningfully spent time.

Work Syncing is not just a strategy or a set of tactics—it's a way of life and a way of operating to enhance your lifestyle as a mindset—it's a decision.

It's said that more than twenty thousand people gathered in Pasadena to see Cal Rodgers complete his mission. His airplane may have consisted of more replacement parts than original ones when he landed, but keeping the plane shiny was not the mission goal.

"The crowd wrapped Cal in an American flag and drove him through the city as thousands cheered. It was a well-deserved hero's welcome. Even more important, America had been crossed by airplane." As the Academy of Model Aeronautics put it, "He had realized his dream." Like gathering for a sunrise or a sunset, people gather to start and complete a dream project.

Sync Your Thoughts and Behavior with Direction and Decision

Work Syncing is an extension of *Final Cause* so you can innovate and streamline at work in a way that values your time and attention to live your priorities and involve others who want to come along too.

Practice Work Syncing by being *project congruent* across (a) thought, behavior, and direction matched with (b) awareness, attention, and alignment.

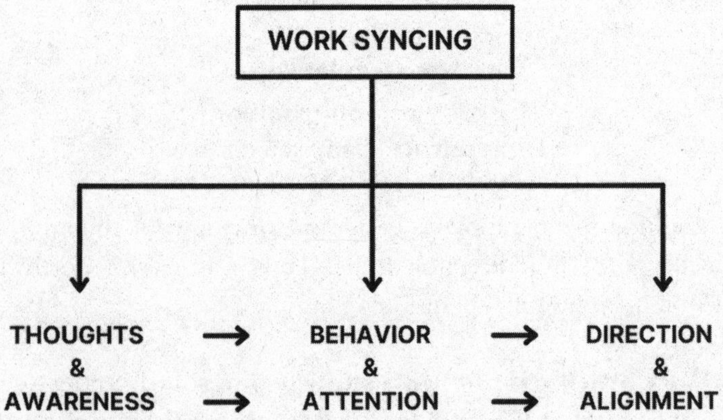

Jeff Bezos Has a Brain Double

. . . and you can too.

When Jeff stepped down as Amazon's CEO exactly twenty-seven years after he started the company, he turned the reins over to Andy Jassy—Bezos's "brain double."

The *New York Times* reported, "Mr. Jassy followed Mr. Bezos everywhere, including board meetings, and sat in on his phone calls, said Ann Hiatt, who was Mr. Bezos' executive assistant from 2002 to 2005. The idea, she said, was for Mr. Jassy to be 'a brain double' for Mr. Bezos so that he could challenge his boss's thinking and anticipate his questions."

You know you're at the pinnacle of productivity when you outsource your brain. All jokes aside, *Expert Sourcing* is as much a matter of how you think as it is the result of thinking. Having a partner, mentor, shadow, consultant, coach—someone to share your thoughts with—is an incredible advantage, especially if you are bringing someone up to eventually replace you in your role.

Apply High-Impact Staging to Work Syncing

John Lee Dumas (a business partner of mine and top podcaster in the world on the subject of entrepreneurship) has a daily podcast. John is super busy—*or at least I thought he was.* I was shocked when he told me how much free time he had.

How could JLD possibly find the time to interview, record, edit, and publish a new episode each day? Well, he doesn't.

» John records fifteen episodes a day for two days a month.

» The other twenty-eight days of the month are podcast-free days.

Rather than slog through the incremental, linear approach common to traditional project execution, synced work is condensed into high-focus, high-impact stages, where work can even be accomplished asynchronously.

Work Syncing varies from batching in that someone can batch their work without synchronizing it with their overall purposes, priorities, or time—leaving them with no more available time or productivity than an average workday. The result of effective Work Syncing is more available time. Ironically, many people who sync time spend their excess capacity (additional free time) on more work—but how you choose to spend your extra time is up to you.

Work Sync staging includes selecting, designing, changing, or adapting your work to make space for the way you want to spend your time.

Staging your work for enhanced Work Syncing means having the courage to set boundaries around what you want and letting your work be pliable enough to support your purpose.

My work is done remotely. I sync my work to various timescales from small projects within large overarching projects. When I travel abroad, for example, I'll make it a point to stage time through Work Syncing to meet up with others. By Work Syncing on my trips, I can see most of the people I would normally meet up with professionally over a year in just one week and bank the other fifty-one weeks. Sometimes I'll make it fun by hosting meetups and stacking priorities.

End Symbols of Productivity

Corporate culture is 99 percent work signaling and 1 percent working.

I asked executives for thoughts on what I call *unproductive symbols of productivity* at work (like staying late at the office to show goodwill when the best thing would have been to get the work done on time).

A Fortune 100 company executive surprised me with this answer:

> Leading a team of about 180, I frequently get people trying to make sure I know they are hard workers by letting me know how many extra hours (either directly or indirectly) they are working. I appreciate dedication and commitment,

> but I don't think of this as a mark of being productive or effective for that matter. What they don't understand is that I am asking myself one of two questions. . . . Are they slow and not up to the task to which they are assigned, or are they not asking for help when they should be?

Another executive shared:

> One person thought it was a badge of honor to have the most overtime. I had to tell them that if it happened again, they would be dismissed because it showed they weren't able to do their work. If only employees knew they could regain their lives, please their boss, and be more productive by working fewer hours.

Symbols of productivity are thinly veiled attempts to hardly work while appearing to be hardworking. Work Syncing does not mean misleading people or office-politicking to earn extra points from a corner-office boss. Moral authority is earned, not given by formality.

Work Syncing means you do the most useful thing at the most useful time to produce the highest-value utility.

In his book *Deep Work*, Cal Newport examines the workflow of Adam Grant, Wharton professor and bestselling author. Newport discovered that Grant "stacks his teaching into the Fall semester, during which he can turn all of his attention to teaching well and being available to his students. . . . Grant can then turn his attention fully to research in the spring and summer, and tackle this work with less distraction." In essence, when your work is prioritized, stacked, and synced, your time is organized so that you turn your attention to where it needs to go with less distraction.

Whatever you do for a living (or however you might change the nature of your career), think imaginatively to sync your work to when you work best and to protect your autonomy to live Final Cause.

Work Syncing takes courage and creativity, but you can incrementally make small changes with intention and effort that have a big, asymmetrical impact.

When you're intentional about when you work and on what, you develop a deep and meaningful impact both on yourself and on those you coordinate with to deliver for those who are counting on you.

Work Syncing can harmonize your various projects (and stack them) for compounding returns on value timing.

What to Do with Downtime

Sometimes we feel guilt over having extra or available time.

In many ways, the Industrial Revolution and its aftershocks—even the way we are educated and measured today—are intentionally designed to keep us working and to feel anxious about our time if we aren't.

- » Postindustrial living means letting robots be robots and focusing on your humanity.
- » If you don't like the rote routine of monotonous manual labor—*do something else.*
- » Bank on happiness and be humble instead of playing the zero-sum game of work signaling.

Sometimes we feel like we must fill every second of every day with something else—*dreaming of home at work and stressed out at home with work.*

Time Tipping isn't about what is right or wrong with what you want to do with your time. *Time Tipping* is about allowing you to create within the circumference you choose with greater precision.

There's a term for artists who don't like leaving empty space on their canvas. This term is called *horror vacui,* "a fear or dislike of leaving empty spaces, especially in an artistic composition"—*a fear of emptiness.* These artists feel compelled to fill every "surface of a space or an artwork with detail." When you create space with *time and Work Syncing,* you can choose to enjoy it however you want—in personal passion projects, professional pursuits, with the people you love, doing "nothing," or whatever you want—that's the beauty of the intent of *Time Tipping*—greater flexibility.

End Ghost Stepping

***Ghost stepping* is what I call taking unnecessary steps *(ghost steps)* we should never have taken and the phantom pains associated with getting stuck and living a *phantom life* as a result.** The incredible thing about ghost steps is that there is no need for a list of them—we intuitively know when we have made one when we are out of alignment . . . *out of step.*

Ghost steps create a false reality.

"I've been successful in business, but it's been because of years of hard work," said Dr. Michelle Jorgensen. "I've sacrificed family time, my health, sleep, and more, all for a reward that didn't seem much like a reward when I got there. I was amazing at writing lists. Long lists! That's what I thought being in control of my life looked like." Michelle was successful, but the lists she was writing created a culture of unnecessary steps—*ghost steps.*

So Michelle took a step back. She took the time to create time by identifying Final Cause and then eliminating, delegating, and outsourcing everything on her long list that wasn't aligned. She erased her ghost lists and instead synced her purposes to step fully into her work and life and gain greater control to live them.

Michelle realized that she could still accomplish all her priorities without doing them all herself. She said, "I didn't have to remove those things from my life, but I don't have to do all of them personally. This has opened up space to do the things that are my calling in life, not the busywork of life." By removing ghost steps, she was able to pay greater attention to her calling in life and create space for other pursuits she otherwise wouldn't have time to do.

In fact, Dr. Jorgensen decided to work on all kinds of things she'd had in mind for years by operating differently. She says:

> I've finished my third book and have two more on track to be completed in the next two months. I have a growing social media platform and am starting a cooking school. I am spending time with my family, have created an education center on my homestead that my family helps run, and have helped my kids live out their dreams. All while running that same all-consuming business. How is that happening? Because I'm focusing on life and living it rather than letting life pass me by while I work day and night for success. And the catch in all of this . . . I'm more successful than I ever dreamed possible.

Phantom living (and the associated phantom pain) looks like doing things you don't have to do, but you think you do—letting life pass you by while you work day and night for success. This isn't to say you can't work day and night for success by choice or out of necessity (circumstances vary). Work Syncing is being intentional about the way you work and understanding what is necessary or not based on Final Cause and Work Syncing on purpose—in all seasons of life.

Michelle synced Final Cause to her work and was able to focus on work, life, and the living of life and to expand into dreams that might have otherwise vanished—*like a ghost.*

Time Tip: Purpose before process,
not process before purpose.

Overcome Ghost Steps: What Is a Step and What Needs to Stop?

Ghost steps can show up as to-do lists, but they can also show up as major projects that don't need to be done at all and everything in between.

"Wasting time" isn't a waste of time if it's aligned.

Ghost steps in time management are measuring something and getting efficient at it when it doesn't need to be done at all. Measuring, for example, how quickly someone can shovel when a bulldozer would do or realizing there doesn't need to be a hole there in the first place are all very different opportunities for identifying what a step is and what needs to stop. You can identify wasted time in ghost stepping by asking yourself questions like these:

- What would I do if I had only an hour to get this done?
- What would I do if I could work only an hour a day?
- What would I do if I worked only an hour a week?

These questions (while you may not think they are realistic) help you identify both what is actually necessary to be done and by whom to achieve your ultimate goal beyond the immediate goal.

In fact, if you look at these questions through the lens of Work Syncing, you might find that with proper planning, alignment, and organization, you will think like an entrepreneur or architect or designer where your key role is to make sure means are methodically organized to achieve success asynchronously, not to do it all yourself.

Another applicable question in understanding where your ghost steps are giving you phantom pains and leading you into a phantom life is this:

Does it need to be done at all?

An effective qualifier to this question is to ask which tasks, projects, and roles are aligned with Final Cause (the castle), which ones are not, and then EDO, Project Stack, and Work Sync accordingly (the moat).

How you measure your future success has a massive impact on how you choose to live today.

Work Sync to Make Memories

Dave Lowell was a financial adviser at a traditional wealth management firm building custom financial plans.

He would see his kids in the morning and for about an hour before they went to bed. His wife, Kirsten, dreamed of going to nursing school and becoming a labor-and-delivery nurse but put her dreams on hold to have kids and support him. He realized he had to make a change but didn't know another way to make his family time work with his work schedule.

Dave was presented the opportunity to become a partner in the firm with the promise of equity ownership and high income. It wasn't until doing his due diligence on that opportunity that he realized everything he had worked so hard for was still ten years away. Meaning, he still wouldn't spend more time with his kids, and Kirsten wouldn't have the space they wanted to create for her to do nursing. He looked at the trajectory of their lives and realized that he had to make a change. He quit his job to start a business and was seeking mentoring to find a way to live his dreams.

What good is a custom wealth plan that doesn't create a wealthy life?

Dave learned that he could create a business model in any way that he wanted that could serve both his clients and his own needs through *Time Tipping* and operationalizing through his dreams through the principle of Work Syncing.

Dave says:

> I focused on creating the lifestyle I wanted and wrapping the business model around the dream, instead of vice versa like I was planning to. It freed me up to create the life I wanted right then, instead of waiting. I focused on creating value online and then making sales with people that were interested and created a situation where all my clients are now inbound leads. I live my dream life. I am in my second straight year of six-figure revenue, working about twenty hours per week. Kirsten was able to do full-time nursing school and is now an RN and finishing up her bachelor's degree. I have spent so much more time with my kids than ever before. We can travel whenever we want, and I work with amazing clients and they appreciate what I do for them. I never would have created a business around my lifestyle without the power of *Time Tipping*.

Looking back, Dave reflects, "I had quit my job at the time, so I technically had zero income. Was it a risk? Yes. But it has to be. Progress in life never comes without risk. You have to bet on yourself. It's doesn't have to be an investment of money; it could be time or energy. But 'what' the investment is is less important than the fact that you believe in yourself enough to get results. Making the investment changes you."

Dave continues his Work Syncing by making important matters urgent. He says, "My oldest child is ten years old, and it terrifies me. That means, eight more years until he could be out of the house.

Eight more years to teach him all I know. Eight more soccer/basketball seasons. Eight more Christmas celebrations. Eight more summer vacations. This is a huge motivation for me. I don't want to spend these years working so much that I miss out on this time with him."

What you work on and do is not the key indicator of how much available time you have. How you work, regardless of whether you like the work or not, makes the difference. Work Syncing makes the difference—*an investment worth paying attention to for greater available time and autonomy for you and those you care about most.*

Don't Build Yourself a Better Time Trap

Synchronizing tasks and goals with time and resources eliminates many "ghost steps" that weren't useful from the start. Dave could have easily built himself a better time trap.

Productivity is not a matter of how many steps you take or how many hours you work. In many cases, one hour of engaged work accomplishes the same results as eight hours of "regular work."

» Instead of going through the motions year in and year out, sync your work time with the highest and best use of the moment directly in line with due dates of your professional work, personal goals, and Final Cause.

» By creating highly focused time on priority work first, the adjacent work doesn't get in the way. It gets done along the way or disappears altogether as being nonessential.

» By syncing your high-priority tasks to the most appropriate part of your day, week, or month, you can eliminate time wasters like task switching.

» Pay careful attention to those ideas that keep coming back to your mind. Ideas left lifeless are ghosts that don't just haunt you, they bite.

Work Syncing remedies situations from the inside out and the outside in to collapse time between what you *say you will do*, *what you do*, and *who you are*.

At the crux, if your normal five-day workweek can fit inside one focused day, you save four days and tip time. Not all work may be able to be shortened, but the fact that you're putting your high-priority work first (not last) will clear up time wasters, eliminate task switching, and expand your mental bandwidth. Work Syncing seamlessly eliminates distractions and time suckers with resolve and builds self-trust and group confidence across stakeholders.

"Time and Work Syncing" Takeaways

You don't have to be everywhere at once to get everything done at once.

» Don't wait to "get in the zone" to be productive. Widen your zone so productivity happens without you. (Don't make productivity wait for you.)

» The product of productivity and success in our personal lives is thoughtful, intentional living (and vice versa).

» Intentional living is the art of making our own choices before others' choices make us.

» Symbols of productivity are not productivity.

» Signaling success is not success.

» Access to resources and being resourceful are two different things.

- Sync your goals to your values you and sync your priorities to purposeful projects that will create time, not take time, in the doing of them.
- Every solution creates a problem, so solve for the future problems of your solutions.
- You're in control. Even when you think you've lost control—take it back through proper alignment of purpose and supporting priorities.

Work Syncing creates a sensible space for you, your ideas, your projects, and your dreams. Leverage the method of Work Syncing to help you be more thoughtful in increasing your productivity and available time while living the dream.

It's not about getting out of your comfort zone to reach your goal. It's about widening your comfort zone so far that your goal fits comfortably inside.

SYNC YOUR WORK

Work Syncing helps you create a moat around your time by streamlining resources.

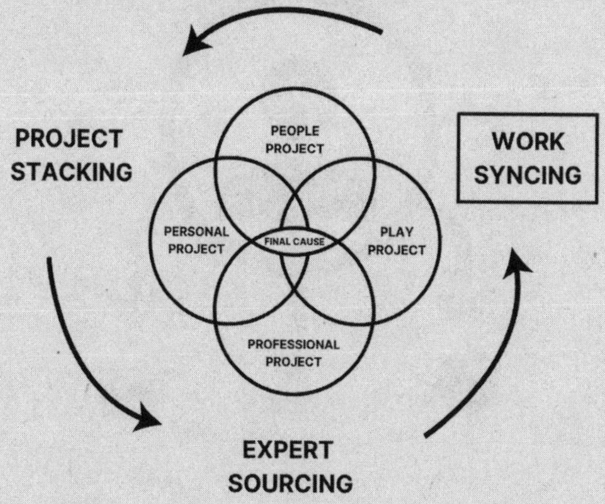

Work Syncing can help you optimize for Final Cause by aligning your projects (and associated tasks, goals, roles) by day, week, month, or year as needed by prioritizing your attention on the high-value activities to reduce task switching and protect your time.

1. Identify what work can most readily be synced together.
2. Sync the work. Pick a day/time that you'll do the work you've decided to sync, and then leave it alone.
3. Go back and do this activity for all of your current work and your Four Final Cause Projects.
4. Avoid the temptation of second-guessing your finished work. That's like checking on the cookies by opening the oven door and letting the heat out . . . Let the work bake properly!

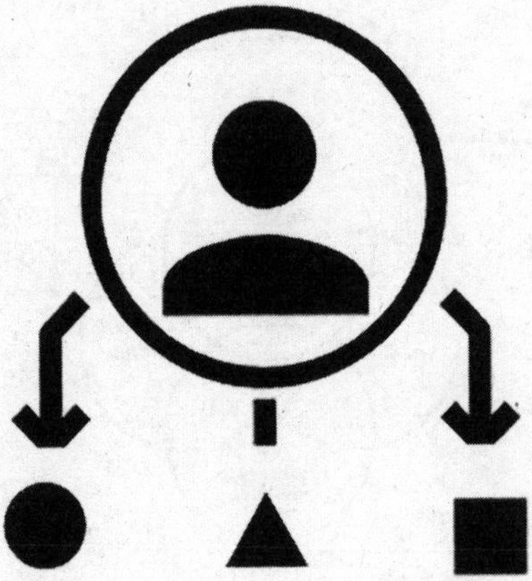

EXPERT SOURCING

CHAPTER 6

Outsource to Experts—Expert Sourcing

How to Do Anything Without Knowing How

> If you know who you are, you'll see where you need to get better and where you might even need to hire someone else who is better than you.
>
> —ALISA COHN, executive coach and author of *From Start-Up to Grown-Up*

There are ships buried under San Francisco.

Thousands of subway riders unsuspectingly travel through a three-masted ship named the *Rome* near Market Street every day. "The *Rome* had arrived in San Francisco's bustling Gold Rush port in early 1850 with a full load of eager '49ers' headed to find gold in the hills, as well as a cargo hold laden with bottles of ale and salt pork." The gold rush brought droves of people from all corners of the world to California, becoming the largest mass migration in US history at the time, and brought a ton of ships.

San Francisco Bay quickly became known as a "forest of masts." Ship captains and crew were searching for gold. The goods the captains brought on the ships became increasingly difficult to get from the deep water to the shore, so politicians decided to bring the shoreline closer to the ships by selling water lots if the purchasers would fill them with land.

James Delgado, a maritime archaeologist at the National Oceanic and Atmospheric Administration and author of *Gold Rush Port*, said, "In order to secure the title, you would put real property on it. You could drive pilings and build a fence around it. But the easiest, cheapest way was to do that with a ship."

Richard Everett, curator of the San Francisco Maritime National Historical Park, explained, "If you scuttled your ship, you could claim the land under it as part of your salvage." Some ships were "scuttled"—intentionally positioned and sunk—while nicer ships became offices, hotels, bars, banks, cafés, churches, and the city jail. Some were broken down for parts, while others were destroyed by fire.

Over time, many ships were strategically built overlaying the foundation of San Francisco's financial district or Embarcadero.

While very few miners struck it rich with gold—*people made more money selling shovels (supplies and services)*—strategic ship captains could lay claim to valuable land with their ships.

Ships are like projects—they serve a purpose until they don't serve you anymore.

Projects are like ships—they can carry whatever you want, and you can anchor them, sink them, burn them, repurpose them, or leverage them as a foundation to build you something else.

Here's the thing:

Captains don't build ships—they sail the seas.

You can spend all your days building ships or all your days sailing seas, and you can do both—but you don't need to know how to build ships to sail the seas, and you don't need to know how to swim to build ships. In fact, oddly, many sailors don't know how to swim at all.

In life and business, it's great to know how to build, sail, and swim, but *being a know-it-all oftentimes stops-it-all* because a leader or a curious innovator lives in the unknown future.

You don't need to abandon your ship to find gold. The value may already be right there on the ship you're on. However, projects serve a purpose. When a project has served its purpose, it's important to become reflexive in the following steps instead of going down with the ship.

Expert Sourcing should become a reflex for you to create time when you feel like your ship is stuck in the dock because you have better things to do with your time.

A sure sign of a lack of self-respect is to keep doing one thing when another would be better worth your time and energy—especially when you're aware of that.

Expert Sourcing looks like this (the shapes represent tasks):

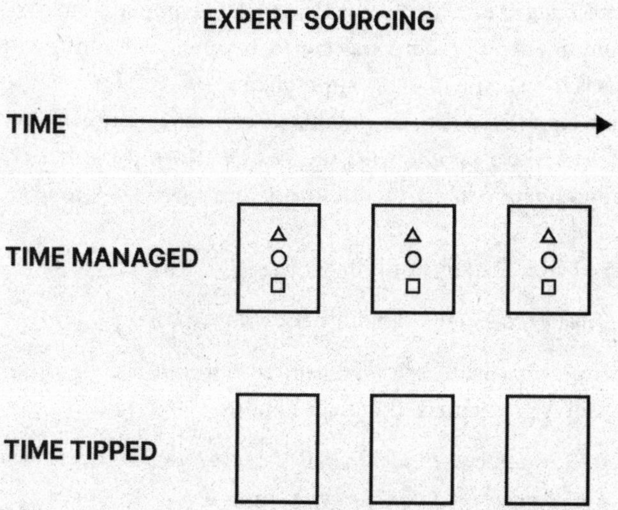

Expert Sourcing to Bless the Lives of Others

Expert Sourcing is the process of gathering experts to consult with or to execute various elements of a project to remove friction and accelerate results.

Getting a job is outsourcing your freedom to a boss, but entrepreneurship is outsourcing your freedom to a hundred bosses.

***Time Tippers* don't trade one job for another—that won't free your time—it will only give you new problems.** You don't have to exchange your freedom for work. You can keep your freedom and get work done differently.

***Time Tippers* don't outsource only to become a manager—that's a self-indulgent nightmare waiting to happen.** Becoming your own nemesis is the recipe of every supervillain.

***Time Tippers* tap into the talents of experts in mutually beneficial ways.** Experts are people who can get the work done better, faster, and even cheaper than you could on your own—*so you don't have to micromanage.*

Here's how Expert Sourcing works:

» ***Time Tippers*** set a deadline for clear results.

» ***Experts*** provide services, software, products, or other resources to achieve the goal. Experts

- *provide results that they agreed to deliver.*
- *provide results on the agreed-upon date.*
- *provide results for the financial amount decided upon.*
- *provide results without oversight—because they are experts.*

Today, talent is everywhere and looking for ways to live independently. You can globally support talented people through expert commerce.

***Expert Sourcing* is a powerful way to reclaim your time and revolutionize life and the way you get your results.** In fact, with the help of an expert, the work will be accomplished better than you could have on your own—*if you would have finished it at all.*

Don't Give Away Half Your Life

When should you Expert Source?

The answer is up to you, but let this question be your guide:

What am I trading my time for?

If your time will be better spent doing something else—*however you define better*—why not Expert Source it? Every moment you get back in Expert Sourcing gives you the opportunity to recover and spend your time on the highest and best use of the moment. More than just giving you the moment, Expert Sourcing can give you emotional strength and mental space from the ongoing bandwidth that comes along with work that crowds your mind.

Don't give up half your life by giving your time to things that don't need you.

Think of the increasing opportunity costs in life and business of doing things that you think need your time and attention to get done, but don't. Your way of life shows up as what you're doing daily but can improve by how it gets done when you're not there.

What could you get done if an expert did it for you?

Avoid Training

Here's the setback with traditional outsourcing:

» Too many hirers try to outsource work and intentionally choose people with relatively no experience that they will need to train and manage when there are experts readily available.

» Choosing to replace one time trap with another leaves you with a harder, more time-consuming job than you began with instead of the goal of zero jobs.

» This leaves the hirer in a position of potentially working twice as long and hard until realizing it would have been better to do the job themselves all along.

This training-required outsourcing process frustrates the one hiring and the one being hired. There is a time and place for training new employees. In Expert Sourcing, you want to work with people who could train you. Hiring someone who already spent years and tons of money learning how to do the task and knows how to do it better than you will help you immediately and save you time without expensive training.

Give Up and Keep Control of Your Art

The Expert Sourcing solution:

» An expert, if sourced correctly, will complete the work faster, better, and *cheaper* than the alternative.

» *Cheaper?* Cheaper is not the goal and often not the best idea. However, yes, cheaper.

» You set the price in an open market of freelancers, and they can agree or negotiate until you reach a price that works for you both.

- If you can afford only so much, you can offer it to the online market and see if there are willing experts.
- Experts will negotiate until they feel they've reached a fair offer.
- When you get the work back from the expert (and according to how you set up the nature of the relationship), you can change, fix, edit, or send back the work for updates as needed.
- When you learn the skill of Expert Sourcing and apply it effectively, you'll get back something that is not only good but better than you imagined.
- When done right, Expert Sourcing will save you loads of time and effort.

Become the director of your own life.

You don't need to do it all. Steven Spielberg doesn't edit films. Michael Kahn does. At a ceremony, Spielberg presented Michael Kahn's career achievement award and said, "This is where filmmaking goes from a craft to an art." Get your life in order by consistently turning your work from a craft into an art through Expert Sourcing.

Expert Sourcing allows you to feel more like yourself again.

Experts Love Work

My mom and dad taught me a metaphor: don't ask someone to dig a hole if you aren't willing to do so yourself. I live by that principle.

You are not giving your trash to someone else to take it out when you're Expert Sourcing. There are many things you don't want to do that other people would love to do for various reasons. There are many things you can't or don't or won't do because you're good at getting started but can't finish or you're good at polishing but can't get started. Someone can help you with that. You're an artist and have a hard time with business, or you're in business, and you need a creative. The opportunities and blessings of collaboration are endless. This is how creative collaborations happen—people working together in harmony, fairly and happily, toward a common cause and with full freedom of choice in how they direct their own time.

Of course, all of this goal setting and doing and cooperating serves the greater purpose of making a deep and wide impact on the world for good and becoming what you want to become. There are billions of people on the planet. You don't think one of them will want to help you at a price you can afford and which is also valuable to them—especially if something that takes you ten weeks (in real time or bandwidth) takes them ten hours or, heaven forbid, one hour?

Welcome to the twenty-first century—the world where tons of people want remote work that can turn into a stack of projects that you can collaborate on together, providing all parties with freedom, autonomy, and choice!

- » Expert Sourcing creates freedom in how, where, and when time is spent for both creators—*the architect and the builder.*
- » Expert Sourcing creates freedom on what projects are congruent with both the inventor and the machinist to their lifestyles.

Few gifts could provide more value, freedom, time, mobility, and happiness to all parties than Expert Sourcing—two or more equals bringing their different talent and expertise to the table and working on some magic within their own zone of happy capabilities.

Give experts work when you can by architecting big dreams that you don't know how to do.

Build Flash Teams

The dream team is a flash team, a bunch of equals with various capabilities combining to make your values show up in the project you started. Flash teams come and go like you might see on the set of filming a movie, depending on the scene and location. With flash teams, you can structure and complete complex work rapidly, without long-term commitments—unless you want them. Flash teams are a great way to test things out while still getting work done in a limited time frame.

My companies have created thousands of jobs through flash teamwork all around the world over the years, making hundreds of different physical products. Big companies are using outsourcing and giving people like you and me the opportunity to work as an expert for them. Crowdsourcing can take a big job, dice it into one hundred tasks, dish it out to a hundred people, and get it back to you in 1/100th of the time it would have taken you to do it yourself—or faster.

Freelancers are the other side of the coin of your projects. In many ways, you and I are both the ones outsourcing and the ones being outsourced to in almost every transaction. On either side of the coin, Expert Sourcing is a great way to be generous, reward talent, create transformational work, and act from your values to get things done at once—without necessarily having to know how to do everything yourself.

Stop Being the Bottleneck

If you ever thought you couldn't do something, now you know you can. You can confidently own your time, projects, and work without being the bottleneck to your own progress and without sacrificing creativity or quality.

Experts who are ready and willing to lend their expertise are perhaps the most undertapped resource available to entrepreneurs, executives, and employees. Rather than reinventing the wheel with each new project or endeavor, get an expert. You can direct your own symphony of experts, events, and processes if you'd like. No excuses.

Freedom rings when you realize you can become what you never thought you could become.

From Project Stacking to Work Syncing to Expert Sourcing

Selling tortillas. Lamar Innes was feeling pretty low. On the outside, it looked like he had it all with a family of four kids and his amazing wife, Chelsea. He had done everything he was told to do. But just out of college and in his first salary job, he was bored, broke, and uninspired. He was working sixteen-hour days, exhausted, and always worrying about bills, but he didn't feel present with his family.

Lamar wanted to control his time, doing meaningful work, and be present with his family. Lamar began to look at things differently when he opened his mind to the idea that he could take control of his time. He didn't know what to do, but he knew something would come if he looked.

Lamar said, "The more I focused and tried to take my time back, it became very evident that I could do anything. I needed to do something that I enjoy doing every day but do it in a way that didn't create another job for myself. I realized I loved food, and I realized that I had been spoiled my whole childhood going to Rocky Point, Sonora, Mexico, every summer enjoying the best flour tortillas the world had to offer. The moment this hit my head, I went to work."

Lamar went to a tortilla factory in Mexico, where he met Pablo and told him he had the best tortillas he had ever tasted and wanted to help him sell more tortillas. Within a week, Lamar had launched a mutually beneficial agreement with Pablo. The "Tortilla Familia" business was born—selling fresh tortillas from Mexico, delivered direct to tortilla-loving customers' homes.

"I wanted to help families have the best possible tortilla through the most effective delivery method," Lamar said.

> The business continued to grow, I quit my day job, we began homeschooling our kids. I was living my dream, owning my time, adding value to families all over while spending quality time with my children. We have been selling tortillas online for four years. We ship to all fifty states in the USA and have thousands of monthly loyal tortilla subscribers. The best part is that Pablo has become a great friend and was able to keep our family business thriving during the pandemic. Likewise, Pablo expressed that our relationship was able to help support his twenty-five-plus employees and keep their business open during the crisis to feed families locally and abroad.

Through the power of Expert Sourcing, Pablo was able to support Lamar and Chelsea's family, and they were able to support Pablo, while expanding possibilities, income, and time for both.

Uploading podcasts. In the last chapter, I mentioned that John Lee Dumas, the podcaster, records only two times a month, but to have those thirty podcasts edited, uploaded, and distributed daily is a lot of work. He Expert Sources that part of his job. Doing so is part of a system (or moat) he created that allowed him to streamline all his work and move from San Diego to Puerto Rico and travel the world without skipping a beat as he lives Final Cause.

Printing and fulfilling journals. After I appeared on John's hit podcast, he asked if I could help him develop physical products. One thing I've helped him create are journals that have generated millions of dollars in income. We make them overseas and then ship them to a warehouse in the United States to fulfill orders. People hear about the journals through his podcast, but many find his journals suggested online. This is a perfect example of how Project Stacking, Work Syncing, and Expert Sourcing work symbiotically to create an abundance of free time, location independence, work mobility, productivity, and money.

Manufacturing and supply-chain operations. Likewise, by way of celebrity example, Dwayne Johnson doesn't physically make the products that he Project Stacks—he Expert Sources the manufacturing, supply chain, and operations. He's not putting shoelaces on sneakers, packaging bottles, or sending out orders in the mail every day. His projects begin and end with him, but his partners and others involved are stakeholders. His businesses are built to scale so they can run without his being there. He can choose to be on-screen—unless it's his body double—or choose to package up orders if he wanted depending on the highest and best use of his time. No doubt he's the hardest worker in the room, *and* he chooses which work to take on, depending on his goal and role. To get work done, he shares the love.

Product creation and prototyping. Pat Flynn and Caleb Wojcik invented SwitchPod through two years of prototyping, getting feedback from video creators, and crowdfunding money to make the first batch. When they approached me with the idea, they had the concept in mind but not the know-how to make it.

Pat and Caleb Expert Sourced their idea to have our team of experts at PROUDUCT work through the details. "We're not a massive company with offices all over the world," they said. "We're just two creators who were annoyed with the options out there to hold our cameras when we film." In fact, the money to go into production was crowdsourced. "We were successfully funded at $100,000 in 12 hours, went on to raise over $415,000 during the campaign, and started shipping to thousands of customers 6 months later." When you're in the hands of an expert, the work should feel light.

Dan Sullivan and Dr. Benjamin Hardy teach in their book *Who Not How*, "What if you had a team of people around you that helped you accomplish your goals (while you helped them accomplish theirs)? When we want something done, we've been trained to ask ourselves: 'How can I do this?' Well, there is a better question to ask. One that unlocks a whole new world of ease and accomplishment. Strategic coach Dan Sullivan knows the question we should ask instead:

'Who can do this for me?'"

Curate Your Life

Thiefaine Magré is my business partner and chief operating officer at PROUDUCT. He is an immigrant from France who speaks fluent French, English, and Chinese. His wife, Maruia, is from Tahiti. They spend their time raising their young children and traveling the world while making their home and living between southern Utah and Tahiti. Thiefaine oversees hundreds of products from various industries and manages the supply chain from ideation to fulfillment. He works globally, remotely.

How?

Arguably, Thiefaine should have no time to live out the lifestyle he enjoys—his supply-chain peers certainly don't have time for much living outside work. Thiefaine leverages the power of Expert Sourcing to support his own expertise by rallying other experts together around a *Professional Purpose Project* through flash teamwork.

Thiefaine explains:

> As business leaders or entrepreneurs we struggle giving the reins over to another person or company. Acknowledging your weaknesses and outsourcing them with qualified vendors, suppliers, or employees is an enormous strength and a formula for destined success. Ultimately you need to decide what you want to do and what you should vendor out.
>
> There is tremendous wisdom in keeping operations lean and managing suppliers that do the heavy lifting for you. This empowers you to continue to focus on what you do best. Once you know what you want to outsource, create a supplier screen, where you define the characteristics of the suppliers you are screening for—namely, capabilities, availability, and relationship. With that you can begin the hunt of identifying potential providers and push them through your screen—ultimately ending with a small group of potential vendors to engage to work for you. This is a dangerous recipe for success! Do what you do best and outsource the rest.

Be the curator of your lifestyle by procuring time solutions for your workstyle.

Are you the Expert Source? It's a weird conversation when people finally realize that their job is to do the work that someone already outsourced to them. You don't have to Expert Source if you like being the Expert Source.

A professional baseball pitcher wouldn't outsource their pitching—they're the pitcher. But there may be a substitute pitcher, a pinch runner, or a pinch hitter to replace work when needed—*Work Syncing stacked with Expert Sourcing.*

If you're a television host and you don't have any time, consider that you chose that lifestyle aware of the urgency created by daily breaking news. Sure, you can outsource all kinds of parts of your job, but if inherently the job requires your face, you either like that part of your job or you don't. You're the expert who has been sourced for the job in many instances.

Don't outsource what you like and want to do. If you don't like the job anymore because it's misaligned with your circumstances, then you can examine the trade-offs and make decisions aligned with your new sense of Final Cause moving forward.

The cool thing about life is that you can make another choice: Are you going to keep doing what you're doing, are you going to strategically quit, or can you get the result another way?

Your new business process. As you move your workstyle from time-managed to anti-time-managed, you'll find grades of opportunity that create more and more available time. *Time Tipping* is a learnable skill set. If you don't want to do it or don't know how to do it . . . *EDO it.* Expand your new time abilities to match your purpose and priorities to create projects with a *Time Tipped* process. Process follows purpose.

Follow the purpose.

You can stay in the race of life as a runner, but always running leaves no time for your loved ones who support you in the stands. Sometimes the most valuable thing you can do is turn the race into a relay and hand over the baton.

I heard someone say that their life changed when they decided to slow down. Their spouse said with relief, "I've been waiting for twelve years."

As a *Time Tipper,* whether you're slowing down or speeding up is beside the point. When you *Time Tip,* you get things done and prioritize without wasting time on things that don't matter. Choose your way out when you don't like what you chose yourself in.

How much time would you have if
an expert did it for you?

Architect your own expert model. Creating time has been my business focus since my brother-in-law Gavin and my son Gavin passed away—Gavin's Law: *Live to Start. Start to Live.* I have a difficult time explaining to people what I do because the Project Stacks are so varied that I sound crazy. However, to me, all my ventures are one: *give people their time back.*

Here's a peek into a few expert Purpose Projects I've stacked around time:

My entrepreneur clients wanted to make physical products, but it was taking up all their time—so I created a service to give them their time back by architecting an *expert model.*

My creative clients wanted to produce videos, but editing took up too much of their lives—so I created a service to give them their time back by architecting an *expert model.*

My executive clients wanted solutions to "starting something stupid" while having the ability to spend time with their families and travel the world—so I created services to show them how by creating their own *expert models.*

These ventures form three legs of an expert *project tripod* of time that give my clients their time back, complement each other, and free up my own time, cash flow, and location autonomy.

How?

These independent ventures are Project Stacked and vary between physical, digital, and knowledge-based products and services. The overarching purpose of the projects (time) serves as a forcing function to create an innovative *purpose ecosystem.* The operations of the projects' *symbiotic priorities* revolve around Final Cause featuring time-abundant methods, processes, and growth space through Project Stacking, Work Syncing, and Expert Sourcing—*regardless of the product or service.*

Time Tippers architect projects in a way that increases personal freedoms while expertly delivering professional results on time—*productivity at its finest.* Some would call this workstyle outcome the ultimate *"work-life balance,"* but *Time Tippers* call this process *"just another day not at the office."*

Time Tipped projects free up your personal time and establish Strategic and Economic Moats around the "castle"—*your Four Purposes,* or Final Cause. You can choose what you want to do, get expert results, and have loads of time by being wise and working with experts. Experts *want* to do the work and are grateful for the opportunity.

"Expert Sourcing" Takeaways

Your ability to do something and your responsibility to do that thing are not the same thing (unless they are).

» The *Time Tipping* method of Expert Sourcing entails a rich blend of proper framing, testing, trust, and transfer of responsibility for a transformational and mutually beneficial experience.

- » Expert Sourcing helps you eliminate, delegate, and outsource tasks and activities for high growth.
- » *Time Tipped* Expert Sourcing is not based on hourly work or micromanaging.
- » Expert Sourcing is value- and results-based work where people use their talents to their highest and best use and meet deadlines without great oversight.
- » Flash teams are used for expert collaborative work in limited time frames.
- » Expert Sourcing nourishes a mutually beneficial ecosystem and generates freedom, money, and time for all parties.
- » Experts do not require training.
- » Experts want to do the work and are grateful for the opportunity.
- » Don't be the bottleneck to your own progress.
- » Let go of your ego and start being collaborative.
- » Architect expert models to recover your time while achieving expert results.

We all have different life histories, careers, and dreams with unique perspectives, constraints, and approaches to life. Be practical. Don't underestimate your ability to take creative control of your time, say *yes* to more happy opportunities, and reclaim your life as you direct the work (not do the work) that you don't want to do—*it's the practical thing to do.*

EXPERT SOURCE YOUR WORK

Expert Sourcing helps you get it all done—even if you "don't have time" and "don't know how," leaving you with *no excuse*.

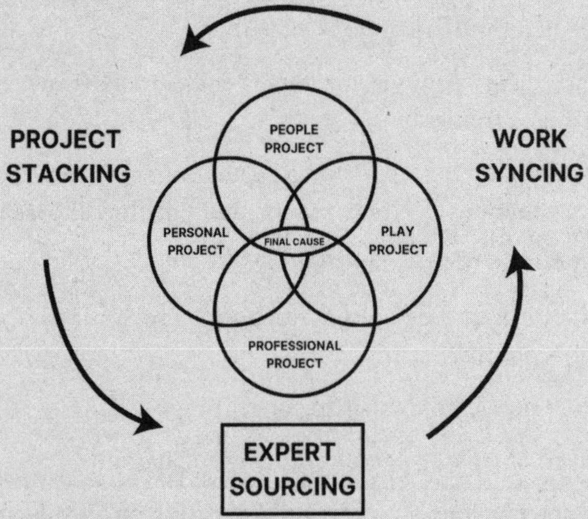

1. Go through your *Time Tipped* Four-*Ps* and the tasks and activities you identified.
2. Look at the list where you identified what needs to be delegated or outsourced.
3. Put a date next to each one where you plan to have that task taken off your plate (if you haven't already).
4. Also, look again at the tasks and ask yourself if it could be done better by someone else (even if you like it, want to do it, and are good at it). What if you delegated or outsourced the process too? Decide on a soft date for the tasks you want to outsource as a mind-game activity to open yourself up to new possibilities. And yes, I mean for you to do this whether you are an employee, executive, or entrepreneur.

5. Using the principles you learned in this chapter, delegate the tasks that can be done by others or that you don't want to do. These are not tasks of your highest use and value. Free your mind and time with *Time Tipped* delegation. Start with one at a time. Build trust with the delegate.
6. Repeat.

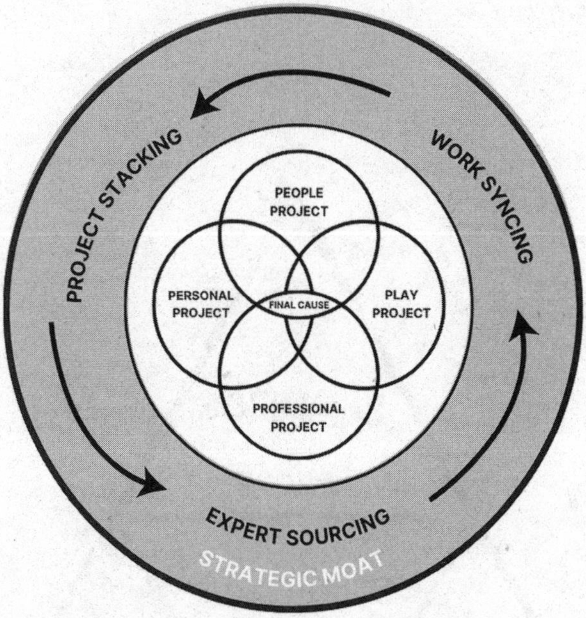

PART III
PAYMENTS

Don't Turn Dreams into Jobs

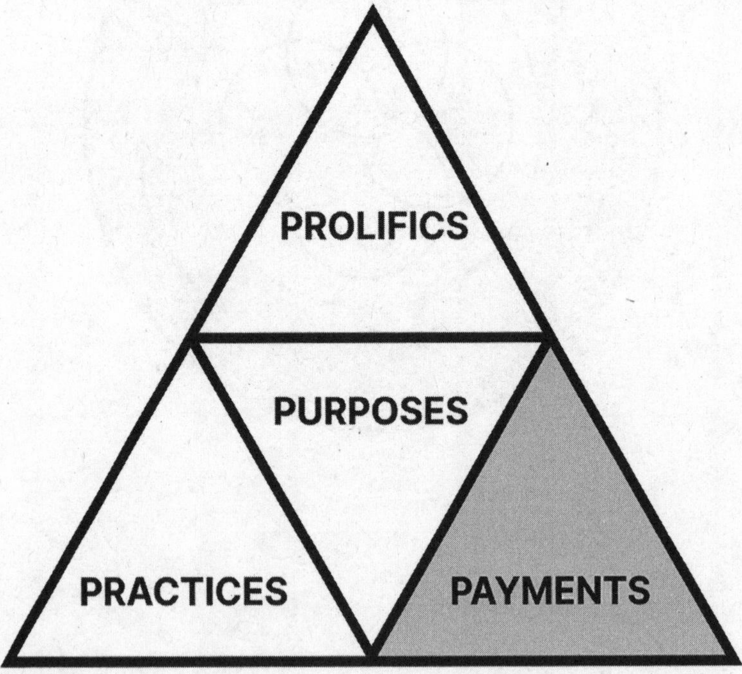

DON’T TURN DREAMS INTO JOBS.

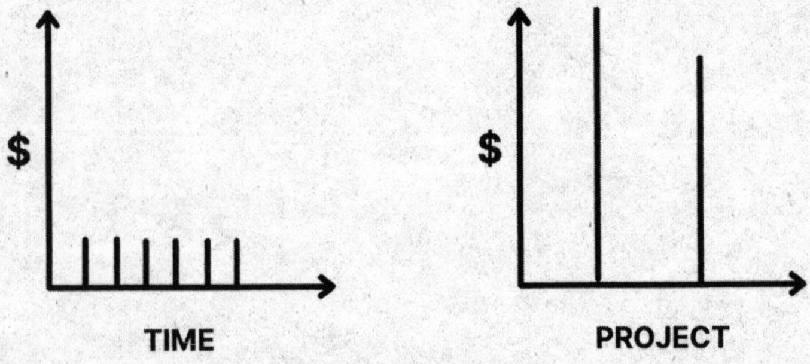

CHANGE HOW YOU'RE PAID, CHANGE YOUR LIFE.

CHAPTER 7

Change How You're Paid, Change Your Life

How to Create an Economic Moat

> The art of getting rich consists not in industry, much less in saving, but in a better order, in timeliness, in being at the right spot.
>
> —RALPH WALDO EMERSON

Laura Wieck says she was "a burnt-out massage therapist with fertility issues."

She was trying to figure out a way to not trade time for dollars. She says, "The best massage therapists are often the ones who spend extra time with their clients (often for free), provide amazing tools and resources for clients, and have a natural intuitive ability to help people 'connect the dots' between what is going on in their clients' bodies with what is going on in their lives." She wanted to help massage therapists have ease and freedom in their businesses, and "that could never be found in the 'time for money' structure."

She asked herself if she could teach massage therapists how to incorporate coaching into their practices in what she calls the

BodyMind Method©. Would they have a framework to work less, earn more, and help their clients get even better results?

Since Laura started the BodyMind Coaching Program, hundreds of massage therapists and holistic practitioners have incorporated this method and have been able to change the way they get paid (instead of single sessions for $100, they now sell BodyMind Coaching programs that range from $1,500 to more than $10,000), and they often share how their clients' lives transform because of this new structure.

Laura describes it this way:

> For me, following my "stupid" idea allowed my husband and me to afford through four failed rounds of fertility treatments and one magical adoption of our son, James. Most important, I am able to be the mom I want to be because I'm not booked solid and exhausted. BodyMind Coaching had been growing, and, in the middle of a pandemic, massage therapists were looking for ways to work that didn't require them to do hands-on, in-person sessions. You helped me look at where I was creating unnecessary steps in my processes while looking at the simple things that could be expanded.

She continues, "In that time, I had my first $100,000 month, which was immediately followed by my first $200,000 month. Changing how you get paid has not only changed my life, it has changed the lives of so many heart-centered massage therapists and holistic practitioners."

Don't Put Yourself in a Box

Hans Christian Andersen would put a note on his table at night before bed that read, *"I only appear to be dead"*—because he was afraid of being buried alive.

Hans—the Danish author behind *The Ugly Duckling, The Emperor's New Clothes, The Princess and the Pea, The Little Mermaid, Thumbelina,* and *The Snow Queen*—understood the value of staying alive and relevant, despite appearing dead and done. It's said his characters and their desperate situations were reflections of himself and his own trauma.

The lessons of many of Hans Christian Andersen's fairy tales show the possibility of transformation against all odds and the nature of how our lives can change. Hans said, "Life itself is the most wonderful fairy tale." Our aspirations, our struggles, our pains shape us—*and so does the way we are paid.* You can transform how you're paid and transform your life.

I'm always doing something different. Like Hans Christian Andersen, I don't want to be put in a box.

Don't put me in a box until I'm dead.

You can change. You can make money in different ways. You can keep your job (or not).

Ultimately, what is it all for and are you willing to put that thing first, now—*before you change how you're paid*—at the center of your life to create work around it as support?

» Maybe your current work situation isn't as ugly as you think.

» Maybe your pride is invisible to you and people are telling you things at work that are not in your best interest only to protect and advance themselves and expose you.

» Maybe some pea-size thing at work is keeping you up at night because someone is secretly testing you to see if you're a fit.

» Maybe you're at a transitional point in life and want a total work transformation—leaping from one industry to another like a fish out of water but with new legs under you.

» Maybe you believe you're too small to overcome big career obstacles, but you want to be honest with yourself, lift your sights, and develop your personal growth.

» Maybe you're too cynical and too cold and take yourself too seriously at work and need to embrace a childlike heart, see the beautiful side of life, and love the people around you.

As Hans Christian Andersen said, "Just living is not enough. . . . One must have sunshine, freedom, and a little flower," and "There's plenty of time to be dead."

Time Tippers focus on creating value that pays dividends in both time and money.

What if you could write the next chapters of your story as the way you want to spend your time?

How autonomous could you be if you changed the way you get paid?

Build an Economic Moat Around Final Cause

Historically, work was locked in *where* we lived and determined *when* we could spend our time on personal pursuits or activities, such as family, travel, and hobbies. In the past and in more traditional jobs, we had to punch a time clock and work at specific times and specific locations. But now, there is far greater flexibility about where and when you can work.

How you get paid—the activities you get paid for and where you physically need to be to deliver the results—***determines your lifestyle.***

» How you are paid is the bond that binds you or aligns you with Final Cause.

» *When you value your time, your life will match your values.*

» How you're paid determines autonomy—the job of a dream is to set you free.

Change how you're paid to intentionally build an Economic Moat that protects your ideal way of living, fuels your time availability, and expands your mobility.

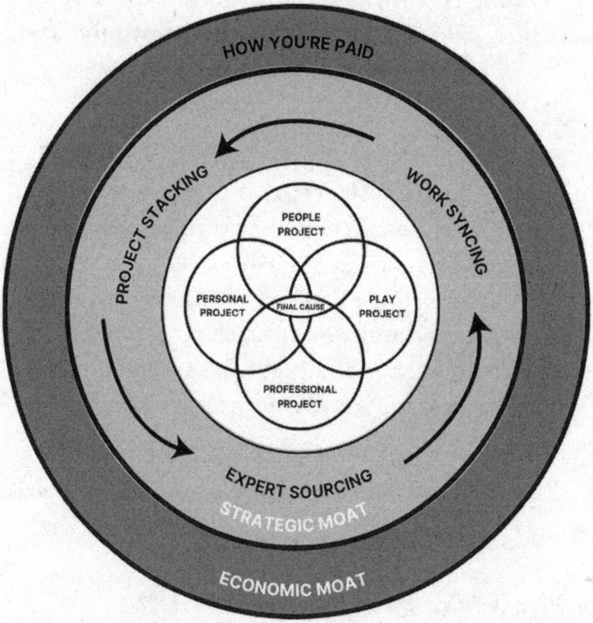

Align Purposes with Priorities with Projects with Payments

Get your power back. It's difficult to live your values if the way you're paid doesn't account for the time or attention or alignment needed to enjoy the benefits of your work.

Ask yourself at the end of the day:

» What kind of atmosphere did I create?

» Is my life in alignment with my values?

» Am I living powerfully through intent?

Building an Economic Moat. To *Time Tippers*, an Economic Moat is created when the professional work you find meaningful supports and enhances your ability to enjoy more and more time and autonomy to live out your personal values.

Changing the way you think about work and how you're paid can be highly counterintuitive but highly congruent to opportunity.

What if we considered this problem through a different lens? What if, instead of trying to fix the visible signs of poverty, we focused on creating lasting prosperity? This may require a counterintuitive approach to economic development, but one that will cause you to see opportunities where you might least expect them.

—CLAYTON CHRISTENSEN

Change How You're Paid, Change Your Life

The Photographer

A successful photographer was trying to figure out what to do with her business during the bitter winter months when there was no work. She wanted to be creative and organize her time so she could continue to produce revenue when shoots work was slow.

After discussing her workflow, dreams, and future, it became clear that she was trapped in a business model that didn't allow her the space to live her ideal life. She needed to change her work-life strategy because her skills and ambitions were bigger than her status quo. I suggested ways she could grow her current business, but also new categories of work she could enter based on her dreams.

She wasn't reaching her highest potential because she did not put Final Cause *first.* She was working on aspects of her business that sucked her time to the point where she didn't have time left to do the things she wanted to do. We shifted her business model from task oriented to value driven and placed her dreams at the center. As a result, her life was transformed.

She identified her Personal, Professional, People, and Play Priorities to support her desired purposes, lifestyle, and contribution to the world. She then built projects around these purposes. Within months of learning and implementing *Time Tipping* principles, she was able to branch out into other income-generating projects that more fully tapped into her greatest passions and gifts. She learned she loved to teach and focused on creating online programs for creatives. In fact, she now runs a seven-figure online education business without sacrificing time to travel with her family. She acted on Final Cause by prioritizing goals and creating projects around them.

Moving from *values* (Final Cause) to *operationalizing values* (Strategic Moat) to getting *paid in valuable ways* (Economic Moat) is the opposite of traditional goal setting and time management.

Time Management:

Find Work → Live Where You Work → Two Weeks of Paid Vacation

Opposite, traditional time and life management begins with payment at the core, which dictates where and how you live, which dictates when you live your personal goals.

Time Tipping:

Values → Choose How You Want to Live → Choose How You Get Paid

The art of creating personal time through professional work is a choice, not a timeline. Placing your values at the center of your life and getting paid for the value produced—*rather than the amount of time spent on it*—is a choice that many have mastered but few take the time to consider after two hundred years of being time managed.

Don't wait until you're "financially independent" to do work as a choice, not an obligation.

The Alaskan Accountant

Casy Price thought she was not capable of living the life she dreamed. She went through the foundational *Time Tipping* process (Final Cause, EDO, Castle-Moat) and changed how she was paid to change her life.

She says, "I made two lists: my tasks and the tasks I enjoyed. I learned I could hire out anything and work with the best. I realized there wasn't competition, only opportunities to work with others and push the boundaries of the typical financial world. I am now living my dreams that were once only in my sleep. Since the world shut down during the pandemic, life around us has been hard, but my business is still thriving, growing, and creating opportunities for others. As a family, we have been able to create memories and adventures on purpose."

Living in a beautiful location in Alaska, their dream was to be able to travel with the family and spend the winter months in Arizona. Casy said that they are traveling in an RV and bought a snowbird house in Arizona. She said, "I love being able to give more," and "I still go back to the basics of my task list when it gets busy again."

You can make a life around your income source (traditional life and time management) or make income sources around your ideal way of life (anti-time management / *Time Tipping*).

The Start-Up Guy

Taylor Cummings was born with six heart defects and given a 5 percent chance to live. After four open-heart surgeries and a couple of miracles, he is alive today and is consistently paced by his pacemaker. Taylor says, "I grew up with a certain passion for making the most of my time. At thirteen, my dad died of cancer. Again, I realized that my life was short, and I wanted to make it count, [and] my thinking changed. Fast-forward—at twenty-two, when I learned I can live my dream and still have my life, I stopped reaching for the traditional entrepreneurial path and wanted to build something around my life." After starting and failing several start-ups, Taylor came up with a model that works.

He said, "At twenty-five, after starting and failing at different things, my friends and I have built a company that takes three hours a week to sustain, and this year we closed our first $20 million deal helping private-equity groups find businesses to buy. I focus on what I love and who I love and have the time to build other things." Today, he is pursuing a PhD in business management and entrepreneurship and focuses on strategic decision-making and performance psychology. He also studied Northern Shaolin Kung Fu at the Shaolin Temple in China.

You can change your mindset, you can change your fitness level, you can change what you read and listen to, you can change all things in your life, but until you act on a new business model through employment or entrepreneurship, your day-to-day lifestyle remains largely the same.

To change your life, you must change how and why you get paid.

The Stay-at-Home, Homeschooling Single Mother of Five Sons

Angel Naivalu was a stay-at-home, homeschooling single mother of five sons, living in a two-bedroom apartment. She completed graduate school in clinical social work before choosing to stay at home full-time. The challenge of keeping up with her obligations at work and home was overwhelming. Where would she find the time?

"I felt stuck," she said. "Time seemed to be the biggest constraint. And the world presented an either-or option: either I could be a stay-at-home, homeschooling mom, or I could be a therapist, working for a clinic, according to their hours of operation. I had no income of my own and felt financially strapped and financially dependent upon my former husband." Angel began thinking through the *Time Tipping* principles.

Angel was able to create a way she could grow clientele purely through referrals in addition to seeing individual coaching clients and hosting sold-out retreats quarterly. Angel's time was freed, and her work had never been more productive or lucrative. Angel said, "Early in 2021, I felt a heart's call to spend one month in Hawaii. 'Who can afford to take a month off of work and vacation in Hawaii?' my programmed brain said. I took that one-month leave of absence from the clinic and spent the entire month in Hawaii. 'Every sunset is an opportunity to reset,' as you say. For thirty days I watched the sunsets over the ocean in Hawaii and experienced a total life reset. Over and over again, I felt my heart say that there was more possible for me on the near horizon."

She says, "My income has increased by 50 percent. FREEDOM!" Angel has since moved to Hawaii and says, "I am in the place that I love most, living my heart's dream of writing and publishing a book, cultivating deeply connected relationships with my sons, earning more money than I ever have before, in charge of my daily schedule, and I feel totally stress-free!"

When you like what you do, you may never want to retire because you're already living like you want.

Work-Life Alignment

Changing how you're paid looks like creating an environment with people, culture fit, and growth potential to match your value and visions of your future.

Making a living relevant and related to your *Final Cause* is an intentional effort to protect your lifestyle by creating an Economic Moat.

The key is to create an Economic Moat that you like to work on and doesn't take time away but creates time while generating income for you. "Conceptualized and named by Warren Buffett, an economic moat is a distinct advantage a company has over its competitors that allows it to protect its market share and profitability. It is often an advantage that is difficult to mimic or duplicate (brand identity, patents) and thus creates an effective barrier against competition from other firms." Likewise, your *Time Tipped* Economic Moat is purposed to give you a time advantage that makes you a powerful asset to employers while simultaneously allowing you to come and go as you please.

The Lawyer

Greg Pesci is a lawyer who had helped lead the sale of a company to a publicly traded company. He was serving as the president but felt that he needed a change in his life.

Greg says, "My family is the most important thing in my life, and I wanted to find a way for my work life to better reflect that fact. I wanted time with my family to be my top priority and to find a work situation that could make that real for me. But I was afraid of trying something new. I had been in the corporate rat race long enough to be brainwashed into doubting it was possible." He wanted to work and get paid in a way that freed up his time around his highest priorities.

As he approached a new chapter in his life, we discussed ways he could stop waiting and start selling to get proof of concept for his new venture to create an Economic Moat around his priorities. Greg shared with me some things he learned in the process:

» "You need to stop trying to get a perfect product or a perfect vertical and do the most important thing early—sell something."

» "Look someone in the eye or speak directly to them online and ask them to pay money for your product."

» "Stop delaying the inevitable. Doing so helped create resources, time, and space to improve our product and, ultimately, to start living the life/work-life that I desired."

The magic happens when you're in motion. Greg's next venture is growing, and so is his available time.

There is no cookie-cutter approach.

Work from the Final Cause, not toward it. Build a business model and sales strategy around your ideal lifestyle from the start and watch your opportunities and time expand.

Live from the dream, not for the dream.

Your Economy

What's the cause and effect of how you work? When people who haven't made money on a project in a long time come to me and want to know what to do, here's the first thing I ask them: *"When is the last time you asked someone for their debit or credit card to make a purchase?"* It gets real super-fast.

HOW TO MAKE $1,000,000

500 PEOPLE BUY A $2,000 PRODUCT
1,000 PEOPLE BUY A $1,000 PRODUCT
2,000 PEOPLE BUY A $500 PRODUCT
5,000 PEOPLE BUY A $200 PRODUCT

500 PEOPLE PAY $167 MONTHLY FOR A YEAR
1,000 PEOPLE PAY $84 MONTHLY FOR A YEAR
2,000 PEOPLE PAY $42 MONTHLY FOR A YEAR
5,000 PEOPLE PAY $17 MONTHLY FOR A YEAR

If *work* to you categorically means that the same work translates to *money*, then you haven't worked a day in your life if you're not making money, are you? You're preparing to work, but you're not working.

Work that translates to money requires sales activities. Working for free or investing time can be a great long-term plan. However, if you need money and your business is not actively asking people in some way to buy from you, how do you expect to get paid? What are you *actually* offering if no one knows what's being offered?

This simple realization that your work practice isn't a money-making activity until you sell takes you off the hook for not making money, *because you're not actively selling*, but it puts you right back on the hook for not making money, *because you're not selling.*

Whether you're getting results as an employee, executive, intrapreneur, entrepreneur, or solopreneur—with strategy, alignment, and implementation you can create an immersive life-work experience you enjoy. Whatever your economic status, your life revolves around how and where and when you work. Identifying this fact can be both eye-opening and empowering.

Be kind and value your time.

- » ***Is this effective?*** Entrepreneurs will pursue a dream with a business to create more freedom and flexibility only to realize that their business took all their freedom and flexibility.
- » ***Is this effective?*** Executives will leave one job for another only to find out the new job has a learning curve that still doesn't provide an improved lifestyle.
- » ***Is this effective?*** Employees will take on a role at work to avoid a bad boss only to find their same bad boss is still actively influencing their day.

Don't let that be you anymore.

Choose a better cause, get a better effect.

Make *Time Tipping* a Daily Interaction

Your new job is to make *Time Tipping* a daily interaction.

While everyone's life is different and the details will vary, the principles of spending time the way you want remain the same.

I learned from the late Clayton Christensen, Harvard Business School professor, to create frameworks *to help others make decisions*—not to tell people exactly what to do.

As you practice *Anti-Time Management* and *Time Tipping*, the answers emerge from the depth of your mind and surface as you integrate the models through experiential learning.

The *Time Tipping Framework*, models, and methods are like a compass where you choose true north to help you navigate the way to where you want to go. Proper alignment with your ambitions is essential to achievement.

Stop living your life with the thoughts you had when you had no time. That project served its purpose and doesn't serve you anymore.

There is no cookie-cutter approach. I've started companies in various countries, consulted thousands of start-ups, poured over thousands of (mostly irrelevant) business plans, worked in venture capital and private equity. I help create (from design to production to fulfillment) hundreds of new products that are sold in the market now or will be soon. In the end, every start-up is different. But in the beginning, every start-up is the same. Or at least it feels that way.

There are so many hopes and dreams and wishes on the line with a start-up, yet there are so many variables in the real world. Even two of the same franchise, just streets apart, will experience different challenges. Anyone can build a business—it's a learnable skill—*building a life you're proud of is also a learnable skill.* Starting a business can totally absorb your time, energy, and brain—*unnecessarily.* Single focused effort is extremely effective if all you want in life is that single thing.

And yet . . .

. . . the depth of life is found in the breadth of living. You need to see more and do more to become more. Life experience is the new work experience.

When you bring your life to work, you bring your work to life.

Variables are constant.

Building an Economic Moat is to personalize the way you work to generate results that pay you in a way that supports Final Cause. No body of work is a catchall. These principles can help you think clearer about what you're thinking of doing, but you must do the work.

Pull a New Economic Timeline into Your Life

W. Edwards Deming, legendary engineer and quality control guru, is credited with observing, "Every system is perfectly designed to get the results it gets."

What system got you to where you are today? This question will help you pull a new *economic timeline* into your life.

There are no shortcuts or work-arounds when you are properly aligned with Final Cause. You inherently bypass the traditional *time-management tease* to open many future possibilities by starting with purpose to catalyze a positive chain of events.

You can pull a new *economic timeline* into your life by considering this four-part process and thinking pattern that many *Time Tippers* pass through as they tip their goal from the end of their timeline to the beginning:

» denial
» survival
» revival
» arrival

At first, you may go into *denial mode* and deny yourself the possibility of success by denying that success is possible. Then you go into *survival mode* and do whatever you've known, or you think will work best, quickly. Then you realize something must change for things to really improve, and you go into *revival mode* by trying new things. Ultimately, you enter *arrival mode* as you find success achieving your purposes. Regardless of where you are at in the *Denial-Survival-Revival-Arrival Loop,* keep in mind the joy of arriving through each phase to avoid discouragement when the path is difficult. Meet each opportunity with wisdom and courage—leveraging the tools of *Time Tipping.*

Choices aren't easy. Choices have degrees of opportunity and responsibility. There's nothing free and easy about freedom and ease. There is nothing easy about the path of least resistance when you consider the opportunity cost.

Rethink Your Rules of Economic Engagement

Three Time Tipping questions. Use these questions for greater autonomy when you create your Economic Moat:

» Will I be paid based on results (not how much time it takes to do it)?

» Will the work be valued at a monetary amount that is worth my time and energy?

» Will I be able to provide the result from anywhere I choose, not a specific physical location?

If the answer is yes to all three of these questions, then the work is likely in line with your Final Cause values, and you should move forward with it.

If the answer is no to any of these questions *and you still want to do the job*, you need to get creative and work through the *Time Tipping Framework* to increase your ability for the project to create time for, not take time from, your Final Cause.

Time Tipping constraints. Apply constraints to your work to design *forcing functions* (forcing conscious attention) to stay aligned.

- When you choose to do work under the scope of your personal values and constraints, you choose to respect yourself and your priorities.
- When work is well chosen, it naturally becomes more important to you and is done with great personal care, resolve, and attention.
- If the work isn't fun or you're having a hard time getting the result, you can *Expert Source.*

You can match constraints to your priorities as a tactic to stay in work-life alignment.

I often find myself discovering positive constraints around my Purpose Projects by asking myself questions like:

- **Is it fun?**
  Do I like and want to do it, so I stick with it?
- **Is it meaningful?**
  Will it help others, so it makes positive impact?
- **Can I do it from my cell phone?**
  Can I be mobile so I can travel?
- **Will I regret not taking a chance on it?**
  How important and urgent is it so I don't miss the opportunity?
- **Will it take away from or support my family time?**
  Does it support integrating my Final Cause Purposes from the start?

Questions like these can help you choose *how to work* on projects that you care about.

Questions around constraints help you design, redesign, purpose, repurpose, negotiate, renegotiate, maintain, update, and operate a congruent work-life process that you're happy about.

Why not have the courage to ask the questions about the trade-offs you're worried about?

Rather than dismantling an old, manufactured process bit by bit to *get your time back*, choose to process your work fit to purpose.

A work process that doesn't serve your purpose now probably won't serve your purpose later.

Positive reinforcing constraints help you scope projects and responsibilities with passion, make deep and wide impact, and free up your time to do as you choose, sustainably.

Break It Down

What are your work constraints for your Personal, Professional, People, and Play Projects?

There isn't a life-work project you'd want to do that you couldn't operate in a way that you desire by making your constraints integral to the process with integrity and creativity. I can say that with confidence because if you choose to prioritize one thing over another, then, with *Time Tipping*, it's done consciously and with respect to higher-order thinking and objectives.

What about stress? One of the more stressful things *Time Tippers* experience while transforming how they work is trying to decide if they should quit their job and how to fill the gap before their next thing kicks in. While every situation is different, one thing is clear: you don't have to quit your job—*if you don't want.*

What if I don't think I can? While some tasks are more difficult than others to change how you operate, the choice between quitting one job and starting a fresh income project is generally an option of desire, not a necessity of function. Reworking your life and business to accommodate for multidimensional living is entirely different from wanting to leave your work.

What about risk? *Time Tippers* mitigate risk in earned income startups by considering ways to *Time Tip* their current work while bringing on new *Time Tipped* projects. Your job is not to add on more projects that take up more of the time you don't have.

What if I don't want to burn a bridge? Before you burn a bridge, consider what side you're on. Bridges don't always need burning.

How can I do more than one job at a time? You don't have to do more than one job at a time if you don't want. Where possible, one of the most rewarding things of running *Time Tipped* projects is the potential of doubling your income (or more) by keeping your current work running as a base and matching that income (or more) with a new project—Project Stacking.

How can I initiate multiple income sources without increasing my work time? Scaling *Time Tipping Projects* that you like and want should be architected under the *Time Tipping Framework* and operated through the EDO method (and the other *Time Tipping* principles) to keep Final Cause at the center of your life to keep your time free.

There is no blaming when you're in control of your time—only realigning as needed.

By the Numbers

Kevin Kelly, founding executive of *Wired* magazine, wrote a legendary piece on moneymaking for creatives called "1,000 True Fans." This article has become a pillar of inspiration and practicality in creative business. The math is applicable cross-industry.

Kevin says, "To be a successful creator you don't need millions. You don't need millions of dollars or millions of customers, millions of clients or millions of fans. To make a living as a craftsperson, photographer, musician, designer, author, animator, app maker, entrepreneur, or inventor you need only thousands of true fans." In short, if you can make $100 worth of profit from a thousand people, you can make $100,000.

How many sales of a $25 e-book would it take to replace your annual income?

For example, someone entering the workforce today may look at the jobs available and consider innumerable options. This scenario could also be a safety precaution against a bad boss or a rainy day as a side business. Change the numbers and apply as needed to suit your situation. Looking at their income options, someone might say to themselves:

» *"I'll max out at about $60,000 a year working for someone else."*

» *"That's $5,000 a month."*

» *"I could make $5,000 a month as a freelancer if I get five clients who pay me $1,000 a month."*

» *"I don't need the benefits—they're inflated—I can look up a local broker who will set me up with a better plan anyway."*

This scenario isn't the future. This is already in the past. There are other considerations such as total cost and special circumstances. Yet apply this example to your own life and change the numbers as needed to see a new vision of what's possible.

Revenue. **The moment you realize that $1 million is a thousand people paying $1,000 is the moment your head should start spinning.**

» The moment you realize that $100,000 is **a thousand** customers paying $100 . . .

» The moment you realize that a $60,000 annual salary is only twenty-four hundred e-books at $25 . . .

» The moment you realize that $25 times two hundred of anything for twelve months is $60,000 . . .

is the moment you realize you could have ten of those tiny ventures making a major dent for good in your life and the lives of others.

Sunk time. If you're dedicating forty to eighty hours a week at work on someone else's dream, what else could you do? If you used the *Time Tipping* principle of EDO and freed up a ton of time, you've also created enough space in your life for a professional side project or stacks of happy new releases on your existing work.

Sync time. How much time and money could you make in your *Time Tipping* practice? What if it were possible to generate enough money, equal to your current salary, without impacting your day-to-day negatively? In fact, what if you could make more money and in less time?

Invest in Your Dreams

My oldest son and his friends planned to go skydiving for his birthday. Raleigh had just turned eighteen, and he was so excited to skydive. I never wanted to go. I'd always been scared and anxious over the idea of jumping out of a plane. But Raleigh invited me to come, and I didn't want to miss out on that cool experience with him.

Honestly, I was okay dying doing this with my son, but the odds of dying were unlikely. We had the best time—one of the highlights of my life. It was an oddly calming and fun experience for me.

As we walked to the tiny plane on the runway, my skydive instructor asked what I did. I told him I was an author and entrepreneur doing international business. He spent the rest of the flight up telling me about his play-to-earn crypto-game income. After seeing the most gorgeous view of Oahu and touching down, my son told me that his instructor told him the same thing.

They were making tons of money online, outsourcing the bulk of the process to freelancers worldwide while skydiving. In fact, they were making so much money and hiring so many people (hundreds) that my son got home, studied it, and started his own account. These skydivers created more financial runway in their lives through their virtual side project than the plane had for taking off and landing.

There are too many ways to live and make money—so pick the one that suits you. This generation, *generation now*, has more opportunities than ever.

Opportunity abundance comes with its own challenges, but it's a challenge you should welcome and participate in.

Be grateful. Millions of people around the world live on less than two dollars a day. Don't spoil your attention span with an ungrateful attitude. Be generous with your time. As we help others with their challenges, we are faced with our own. Keep helping anyway.

Recognize this. If you have a blatant disregard for your time, so will everyone else. You are a natural resource that corporations will deplete, if allowed. You wouldn't be the first to lose your best years to the company. It's up to you to replenish your time.

Given a choice, which you are, what would you do with your time? Where would you go? How would you be paid? There are so many opportunities to switch it up.

Modern work is shifting to contractors and entrepreneurs, and corporate is switching to automation. The opportunity to match corporate work with freelancers and freelancers with corporate work is gigantic. The opportunity for you to carve out your own space in this world doing things you like with those you love is yours to take.

You gotta make it a priority to make your priorities a priority.

Are you paying attention?
Attention will pay you if you want
to participate in the new global workforce.

"Change How You're Paid" Takeaways

There are tons of ways to make money, yet regardless of how much you're paid, how you get paid dictates your lifestyle. Reread that last line. Internalize it. This is important because even those who leave jobs to become entrepreneurs mess it all up when they create another job for themselves.

» The good news? The gospel of pay is that you can change your life by changing how you're paid.

» Your way of living is directly tied to how you are paid, where you are expected to be, and how you deliver on that obligation.

» The modern job is a relatively new creation in history. Be wise. People sitting all day looking at a glowing light are bound to get run over like a deer in headlights.

» *Time Tippers* create enormous value for one person rather than minimal value for several, so you do better and free up tons of time that you can then dedicate to other things.

» If you want to work for a company, your job is to leverage the *Time Tipping* tools on your work to reclaim your life—*how you work* (not necessarily what you work on) makes the difference between how much autonomy you enjoy.

» If you're in business for yourself, your job is to earn the trust of more paying customers or clients as a result of your *Time Tipping Projects.*

» If you want to learn more about a career or industry or project, your job is to earn (not get) mentors as a result of your *Time Tipping* resolutions.

As you change how you're paid, you gain greater control over your castle by building Strategic and Economic Moats around it to protect your interests. Center your life by wrapping your arms around your *Four Purpose Projects* and hug out your Professional Priorities to support your Personal ones. *Time Tip* a process that gets you paid in a way that affords you new freedoms to help more people.

Changing how you're paid looks like this:

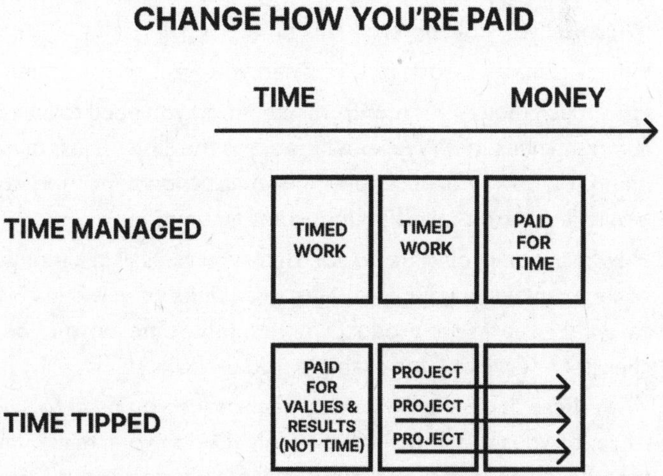

CHANGE HOW YOU'RE PAID

***Your turn.* This activity will help you think through your choices to change *how* you get paid to change your lifestyle and help you move from making goals to making decisions:**

BUILD YOUR ECONOMIC MOAT

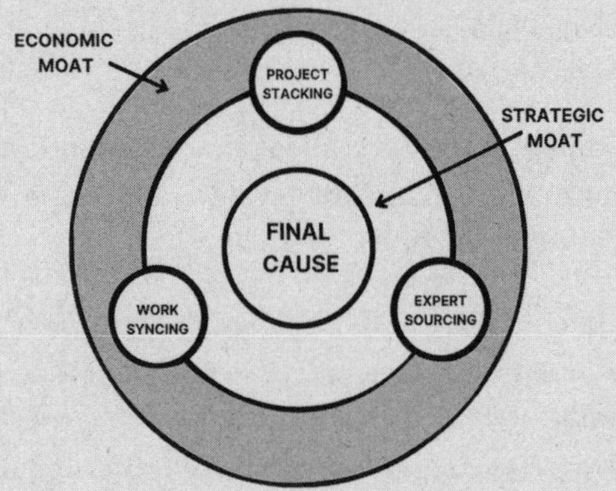

1. Acknowledge that you have a choice in how you get paid (not easy, but a choice nonetheless).
2. What has stopped you from living this way before?
3. What will you do differently this time?
4. What meaningful work (projects) do you want to get done?
5. How much money per month, minimum, do you need to make it worth your time? (We know the sky is the limit . . . just minimum for now—for example, how much money per month would it take to replace your current income?)
6. How many units of value do you think you can sell in a month while maintaining your ideal lifestyle? (Units of value, in this case, may represent products, hours, jobs, time on the job, clients, or services—for example, 100 e-books.)
7. With these numbers, what price per unit do you need to sell to reach your monthly financial goal? (Divide your minimum monthly revenue goal by the number of units to see the price

point you'd need to sell at—for example, $5,000/100 e-books = $50 price per e-book to reach your revenue goal.)

8. This is a starting point. Change the numbers as needed. The principle is to keep your priorities and lifestyle at the center and then build a business model around it that works.
9. What decisions (with deadlines) will you make to *Time Tip* your reality?
10. Fill out this one-page business model optimizer to help you think through different ways to get paid.

CUSTOMER (PURPOSE)

PROFILE: WHO IS YOUR IDEAL CUSTOMER?

TARGETING: WHERE DOES YOUR IDEAL CUSTOMER HANG OUT?

MARKETING: HOW DO YOU REACH YOUR IDEAL CUSTOMER?

VALUE (ATTRACTION)

VALUE PROPOSITION: WHAT'S YOUR BIG PROMISE TO THE CUSTOMER?

POSITIONING: HOW DO YOU DIFFERENTIATE FROM COMPETITORS?

DISTRIBUTION CHANNELS: HOW DO YOU DELIVER ON YOUR PROMISE?

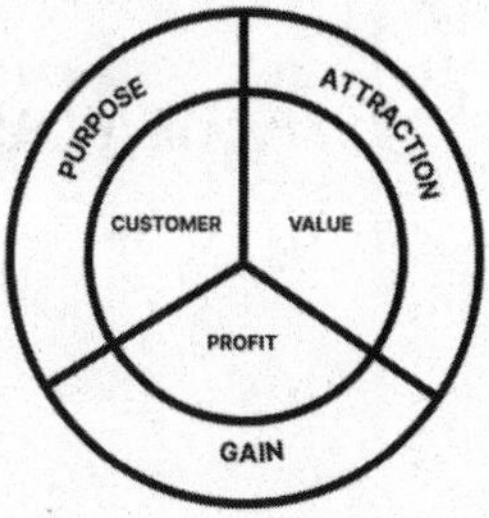

PROFIT (GAIN)

PRICING: WHAT'S YOUR PRICING STRATEGY TO MAXIMIZE PROFITABILITY?

REVENUE STREAMS: WHAT METHODS WILL BE USED TO GENERATE REVENUE?

CONTRIBUTION MARGIN: HOW MUCH MONEY DO YOU MAKE PER UNIT?
(CONTRIBUTION MARGIN = SELLING PRICE PER UNIT - VARIABLE COST PER UNIT)

VALUE YOUR TIME, DON'T TIME YOUR VALUES.

CHAPTER 8

Value Your Time, Don't Time Your Values

How to Do What You Want When You Want

> I've become convinced that time management is not a solution—it's actually part of the problem.
>
> —ADAM GRANT, organizational psychologist

When I was sixteen, I really wanted to start making my own money. I thought the best way to do that in my small town was to get a job at the grocery store or gas station or pick up trash at the county fair. I told my dad I wanted a job, and to my surprise he said, "You don't want a job." I asked why not, thinking that getting a job was a super-responsible thing to do. He told me that I'd be working my whole life and right now I should focus on school and having fun. But I persisted and explained I wanted to be able to make and spend my own money for more freedom.

He then came up with the most random plan.

He told me to go to the watermelon farms and ask if I could buy all of the irregular-size and -shaped watermelons. He said that the farms couldn't sell them to the grocery stores. They'd go rotten and be thrown away.

My dad gave me "seed money" to go and negotiate for the watermelons. My younger brother, Erik, and I drove to the farms in El Centro from North County, San Diego, California. We took out the backseats of our family van and bought enough watermelons to fill it all the way up—about a hundred watermelons.

When we got home, I reached out to neighbors and friends' parents and told them that we had weird-looking watermelons for sale. I told them they were delicious and cheaper than the ones at the store. It was almost the Fourth of July, and Erik and I set up a stand at the park so people could come pick them up while we sold them to anyone walking by who could heft a watermelon around.

Erik and I sold out! We made more money than we would have made the entire summer working for minimum wage in a few hours. I was planning on giving away my summer, but my dad thought differently about time and money.

When I think back on this experience, I think it was a turning point that changed the trajectory of my life.

» I learned I didn't have to trade time for money.

» I learned I could think way outside normal patterns of thought to achieve a goal.

» In this case, having money and the freedom to spend it didn't have to look like a job.

I believe it was this experience and others that helped shape me to have a mindset where my family and I can travel the world, take in foster children, and work on passion projects that don't have anything to do with money at all.

Likewise, you have experiences that help you see a bigger picture that creates your moral compass. Be compassionate when other people can't see your bigger picture. **When there is a fast, traditional answer right in front of you, it's really hard to see a different solution—even if it's wiser.** That's why today I'm so willing to share and be transparent about what's working and not working today based on the well-being interests of my community now.

The answers to the problems we are solving today simply aren't found in books—not even this one—or on the Internet. The answers we are solving for are so individual that you have to think and act for yourself. Teaching principles and integrating across models for expansive thinking and problem-solving help people solve their own problems better than waiting for the solution to appear. Your life is filled with people who can mentor you in person, online, or by way of example. When you read and listen to people and their stories, look for ways to apply your values to your situation by drawing from their wisdom and experience—like how my dad taught me how to make money without getting a job.

Time Management Work-Life Value Misalignment

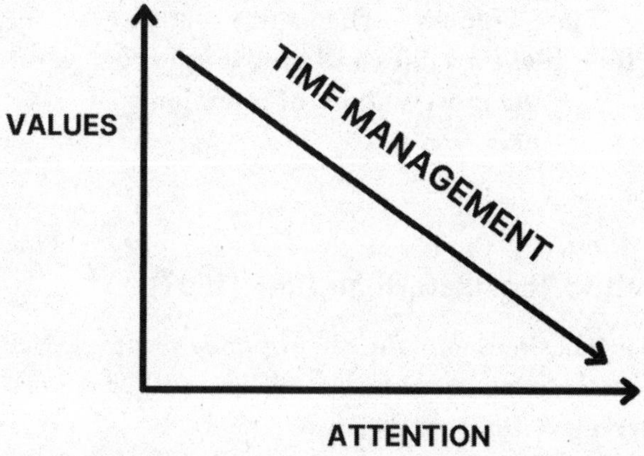

Time management ignores personal values, making one's personal highest values and priorities receive the least amount of attention. Further, time management often spends enormous amounts of time on low-value projects because of a mismatch in measuring efficiency over effectiveness—churning out mediocrity in both business and life.

Time Tipping Work-Life Value Alignment

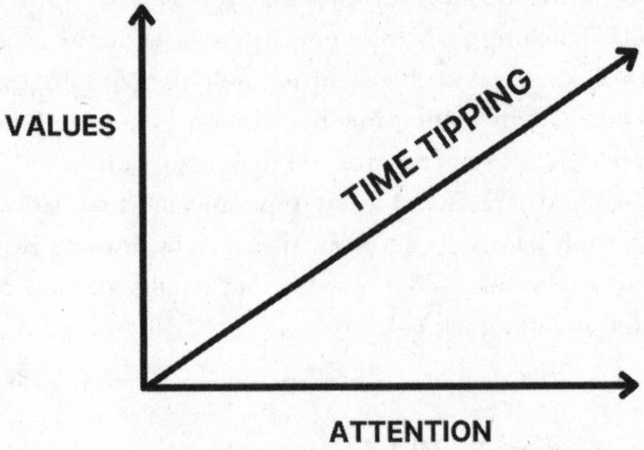

Time Tippers work in a way that allows their highest values and priorities to receive the most amount of attention.

Get a Positive Time Return on Time (TROT)

I asked Marshall Goldsmith, the number-one executive coach in the world, about the relationship between being satisfied at work and at home especially during times of chaos.

Marshall told me, "We did a study of how satisfied [people are] with life at work and at home. And we found out that people who are miserable at work, tend to be miserable at home—because it's the way they approach life itself." On the other hand, people who were satisfied at work and home weren't "waiting for the company to make them happy . . . they provided for themselves at work or at home. . . . People get in the habit of being a victim at work or a victim at home." He says that what's important is to ask, *"What can I be responsible for?"* You can't necessarily solve everybody else's problems, but you can certainly work on your own.

Goldsmith continued, "You do not become ego attached to results. Why? You don't control the results. Results are a function of many factors. Some you control, some you don't. You don't have your ego attached to results. You let go of what you can't change. You let go of the past, you focus on what's in front of you. You have a plan, you execute, you do your best. And you repeat the process."

Goldsmith's study on work-life satisfaction found:

> Overall satisfaction at work increased only if both the amount of happiness and meaning experienced by employees simultaneously increased. This indicates that professionals don't gain satisfaction at work either by being "martyrs" or by "just having fun." Companies may want to reduce communications designed to encourage employees to make sacrifices for the larger cause. They may also want to cut out "fun" morale-building events that lack a meaningful purpose. We had (mistakenly) guessed that those who spent more time outside of work in activities that produced more short-term satisfaction might score higher on overall satisfaction. After all, we assumed, people don't go home to find meaning; they want to relax. We were wrong. The correlations between happiness, meaning, and overall satisfaction at work and home were very similar. Those who were more satisfied with life outside of work were the respondents who reported spending more time on activities that produced both happiness and meaning.

You don't need to be a martyr for your personal or professional pride. Be humble and pair your time with living your values.

» Talk about the lifestyle you want that will come from the work that you do.

» Don't keep it a secret.

» Take that dream and bake that into your business model right now.

Don't time your living in preparation to one day live your values.

Is purpose embedded in the culture of your dream?

You Are Cementing Pathways (for Better or Worse)

Living through the life-quality lens of Final Cause can change the way you approach everything and arrive with greater contribution, fulfillment, and success.

Values are inextricably linked to purpose.

One of the most difficult things for a founder, manager, or leader is to scale a business when bottlenecks prevent seamless growth. Bottlenecks are made by design, default, or demand. If you want to scale, it can make sense to *build to scale* from the start by baking in your values without introducing unnecessary, preemptive, or burdensome costs. Operating for the sake of the ultimate outcome from the start can look like metaphorically structuring your process with bottles without necks (or no bottles at all) for what you value most.

> The foolishness of continuing down a wrong path after you've already discovered its negative ways is called pride. Humility is doing what's right when it's hard and turning around when it's wrong.

What would you do if there wasn't a bottleneck? Do that.

Whether you're a *Time Tipping* entrepreneur, executive, or employee, or for everyday living, remember that what you're doing today is cementing pathways that will be used tomorrow. The high switching costs of turning cement pathways *(how you do your work, routine, habits, process, policy, and procedure)* into something that they are not *(your lifestyle, your family time, travel, the meta-goal, freedom, autonomy)* is expensive and sometimes impossible.

> Sometimes the best exit strategy is creating something you never want to leave—but you can whenever you want without skipping a beat.

Become It Before You Become It

A busy executive contacted me and said he's making $250,000 a year. He can't handle the time constraints because time is slipping away as his kids get older. He needs more freedom. The money's great, but there's no time, so what's it worth? He wanted to leave the job and start two gyms.

I said, "Look, this could make a lot of money. That's great. Are you telling me that freedom to you means when you go to bed at night, you wake up and wonder if the door was locked because you're managing gyms?"

I continued, "You want freedom with your kids who may be thirteen now and will be eighteen in five years. You think that in five years, you'll finally have freedom from the grind. But during that time, your kids will have grown up and left. Is this the business that will give you that freedom today, not tomorrow?"

He realized that this wouldn't be the next gig for him unless he hired a manager and outsourced the operations to a team that he would hire. He didn't want to outsource, however, because he considered himself a micromanager and wanted to be there.

Again, what you do is less important than how you do it to create *continuous autonomy* and freedom of time.

Many people are not willing to do the work because they are very controlling and would rather work unproductively and out of alignment than find solutions in ambiguity. People can choose whatever dreams they want, working night and day on them. Just don't fool yourself saying *"This work is going to get me my dream"* if it won't. While most things in life are totally out of our control, *Time Tipping* gives you space in ambiguity to assess the decisions involved to help you choose how you want to show up in any given situation.

The way to become who you want to become in the future is to become it in the present.

Become it before you become it to become it.

Move from Continuous Dreamer to Fulfilled *Time Tipper*

Avoid hollow hopes. A common problem in working for time freedom is working in ways that don't provide it and never will. It's a difficult path for people who say they have dreams when they make choices directly opposite of the dream. Actively acting on activities that will not get you closer to your dreams are what I call *hollow hopes.* Hollow hopes happen when people would rather hold to the dream (to maintain hope) than risk working for the reward (in fear of losing hope).

Don't be a dream dodger. In surfing, the term *barrel dodger* refers to someone who misses the "barrel" (or "tube")—*dodging a hollow wave.* Likewise, people will prepare to live a dream, but at the most pivotal moment will turn away instead of pulling in. Don't dodge dreams. To live dreams: pull in, be encapsulated, and tip time.

To avoid hollow hopes, you have to fill the void with the right activities.

Remember: Your life should consist of more than commuting, working, eating, surfing the Internet, sleeping, and watching TV. Your life should be filled with purpose-driven experiences and projects that bring excitement, passion, energy, and authentic meaning and joy into your life.

Make Money Devoted to Values by Thinking Algebraically

Don't be the problem to your own solutions.

When you separate yourself from the equation and ask, *"How can I get this desired result without doing the work I don't want to do?"* you create solutions that allow you to put yourself back into the equation, flexibly—*if you want and as you see fit.*

Our minds are like calculators, but they don't calculate rationally.

What you think is what makes something possible for you, or not. You won't even try to solve for problems that you don't think can be solved.

Instead of saying, "I can't do this," think algebraically.

Ask yourself:

"How can I do X, without Y happening, by Z time?"

Thinking algebraically helps you analyze patterns, relationships, and how things change. You may not have the answer now, but by asking algebraic questions you create space in your mind for the solution to emerge.

Have you ever had an answer come to you while you're running or doing the dishes or in the shower or driving or on the train, and so on? Your brain was working in the background. Encourage your *Time Tipping* brain by asking better questions.

Algebraic questions are more effective in solving problems than approaching a problem with *"I can't do this because . . ."*

Why would you shut down your creative thinking machine when it wants to solve the problem without hurting your ego? You're smarter than you think, and your brain is capable of solving complex problems with elegant, simple, practical solutions. Open your brain up to allow for new inputs that can create greater outputs with better questions. Simplicity is complex. It's never simple to keep things simple. Simple solutions require the most advanced thinking.

Are you giving your brain some space to think instead of telling it what to do?

Build Your Own City

The challenge is that the old brick-and-mortar, micromanaged, job-for-life mentality is what we've built cities around. Literally. Cities are built around this three-step model:

1. Here is where people will work.
2. Here is where people will live around work.
3. Here is where people will commute to work and back.

Only, today we don't need to live that way. The brick-and-mortar mentality is outdated. Keep it simple.

In a world where you can live where you want, work from anywhere, and come and go as needed . . . are you? The concept of sitting in an office and in front of a computer screen from 9:00 to 5:00

is perhaps the worst working environment for creative and innovative ideas. Does it work for industrial workers making widgets? Probably. But unless that's your business model, it's time to rethink your aversion to remote work. If you're an employer, it's time to rethink your aversion to full-time remote employees (and not practicing *digital Taylorism*—micromanaging their every move virtually is going backward).

Security comes from knowing who you are and being willing to fight for that thing.

Getting financially fit doesn't have to come at the expense of your way of life. If you choose a side project, contract work can be great because you can take on multiple jobs (as many as you want to handle or delegate). You can be free from the confines of the cubicle (the highest form of payment is freedom).

Look for companies or talk to your manager at work about delivering results remotely. **When you work in this capacity, you'll be blown away at your hyper-engagement to the business—*because it is your business.*** It just so happens that you may be doing it from your cell phone on the top of a mountain or on a boat in the middle of the ocean. That's a good thing.

Charge High

When Tesla announced their $35,000 car, it was a weirdly massive price drop from their prior models that sold for more than $100,000. Why would they drop the price so dramatically? On the surface, the decision felt like the opposite of conventional wisdom.

Most people start with cheap offers to "get you in the door," so eventually you may be interested in the high-tier offers. However, it was Musk himself, years earlier, who wrote the following.

The master plan is:

Build sports car

Use that money to build an affordable car

Use *that* money to build an even more affordable car

While doing above, also provide zero emission electric power generation options

Don't tell anyone.

Instead of having to produce mass amounts of cheap goods, Musk was able to use the funds from his high-priced cars to a small audience to fund lower-priced ones to a large audience. Additionally, the higher-priced cars helped Tesla gain attention, exclusivity, desire, and their audience/fans.

Then, after patiently waiting and building brand reputation, they rolled out the lower-priced model that everyone wants at the critical point of mass exposure. Note: You do realize there are plenty of other electric cars similarly priced as the Tesla Model 3, right? But apparently, no one wants them now.

Let that sink in.

Elon Musk said, "I think it's very important to have a feedback loop, where you're constantly thinking about what you've done and how you could be doing it better." Most entrepreneurs start with low-ticket items offered to a small audience and wonder why they end up failing with "cash-flow problems." With confidence and foresight, start with high prices. Go big. You're better off working with one client for $1,000 than ten clients for $100.

But most entrepreneurs don't do this.

Instead, they work crazy hours making pennies! Why? Fear. They aren't willing to swing for the fences and play the long game. If you create enormous value for one person rather than minimal value for several, you do more good and free up loads of time you could dedicate to other things.

You can do this right now. It all starts in your head. But what goes on in your head dictates your reality.

Do you have the gumption to swing for the fences and play the long game? The simple formula:

» Build a high-ticket offer.

» Use that money to build another high-ticket offer.

» Use that money to build another high-ticket offer.

If you have a potential client base of a hundred people, target the one to five who will love the biggest thing you can offer. Forget about "selling" the other ninety-five to ninety-nine right now.

That's what Musk did, and people love it.

At the same time, remember to give the ninety-five to ninety-nine who aren't ready to buy (at the high-ticket level) great value through free offers and nurture the relationship (through e-mail, community building, and social influence) to prepare them to work with you on a deeper level.

Once you get traction, which comes more authentically than you think, you'll have loads of freedom to focus on low-ticket expansion if you choose.

Freedom, influence, and impact first. Expansion second.

Or you could keep doing what you're doing . . .

Value Your Time by Not Needing to Have All the Skills

You want to perform at great professional heights and enjoy it while also enjoying your personal roles at home and play.

High performers don't have all the skills they need, and so they have to live differently, embracing what they want to do and Expert Sourcing what they don't (or can't) to live their values and change how they're paid.

At the end of the day, if you can do it all by yourself, why would you? If going solo is 100 percent the best way for you to do it, then so it is—you also have zero to complain about because you already understand the time consequences that come along with doing it all yourself.

You're not a machine.

Is it weird that we must remind ourselves of that?

Look up. Right now. What do you see?

All that stuff around you was made and sourced by someone after someone else blueprinted it. You can do that too.

Change *When* You Prioritize (Not What)

Practicing priorities is different from having them.

Your priorities may be in order in your head, while in practice they are out of order—like millionaires strapped to a chair by choice because their business model revolves around the revolving chair they sit in.

Want to live your priorities?

Change *when* you prioritize, not what, and watch your priorities happen in real time.

You're Not Too Late

Cameron Manwaring was struggling and had cautiously stepped away from a growing multimillion-dollar company because of a divorce. He was terrified. He felt that he had lost years of experience and progress.

I shared with Cameron the principle of experience that Stephen M. R. Covey once taught me—*"Some people say they have twenty years' experience, when, in reality, they only have one year's experience, repeated twenty times."*

Cameron said:

> From that point on, the fear that I had "wasted away" years of my life in a bad business or a bad relationship vanished. I had full confidence that I could gain twenty years of experience in two years with the proper mindset and focus. Ever since, I've purposed my time accordingly. Always be careful to never allow myself to be "busy" instead of focusing on outcomes and results. As such, I've rapidly changed the direction of my life! I now am married and have two beautiful children, and in the last year, I've generated more personal income than I did the first five years of my previous company.
>
> *Valuing your time instead of timing your values is not a matter of age or circumstance. It's a matter of choice and determination.*

"Value Your Time" Takeaways

If you're ready to revolutionize your lifestyle, here are some quick tips for creating *value timescales*, flexibility, and freedom for yourself:

- » Choose work that gets you excited.
- » Start a project independent of anyone else.
- » Invite influential people and organizations that you'd like to work with to help you complete your project by a certain date.
- » Build a business model (ways to make money) around a successful project that integrates the expression of your values.

You deserve to live in a way that can create money, meaning, and freedom to live life on your own terms, no matter the circumstances. Working to make an extra $1,000 by selling a $1 item causes different time constraints (a different lifestyle) than selling one thing for $1,000. Remember: It's not about getting out of your comfort zone to reach your goals. It's about widening your comfort zone so far that your goals fit comfortably inside.

VALUE YOUR TIME, DON'T TIME YOUR VALUES

This activity will help you self-reflect on how you're valuing your time to help you reprioritize, rework, and reignite joyful living.

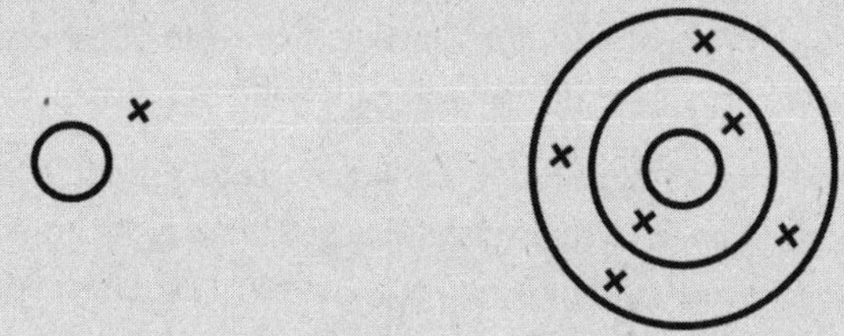

IT'S NOT ABOUT GETTING OUT OF YOUR COMFORT ZONE TO REACH YOUR GOAL.

IT'S ABOUT WIDENING YOUR COMFORT ZONE SO FAR THAT YOUR GOAL FITS COMFORTABLY INSIDE.

1. What do you want to do to align your time and money with your values? Not all of these questions will be applicable, but think about how each applies to you and people you know.

—*When* do you get up in the morning? Why?

—*When* do you come home? Why?

—Do you have to ask someone for permission to do anything, anytime, ever? Why?

—If you had a different job, would your lifestyle change . . . at all? Why?

—*Where* do you live? Why?

—*When* do you go on vacation? Why?

—Do you dread Monday, or is it like any other day of the week? Why?

—*Who* do you hang out with 9:00 to 5:00, Monday–Friday? Why?

—Are weekends a break for you? Do you like them or dread them? Why?

2. Note: These are all loaded questions tied directly to *how* you do your job and *how* you get paid. *Not how much you get paid. Time Tipping* is a learnable skill.
3. Go back through the questions, only this time ask yourself what you'd like to be doing instead. Where things align, you're aligned. Where they don't, make room for questions. This is an inventory of today so you can make decisions.
4. If you see something you'd like to change, don't attach an emotion to it. Simply ask yourself how you could create change while still fulfilling your current responsibilities.
5. Choose one value to being with that you'd like to integrate better with your life.
6. Now, go tip time!

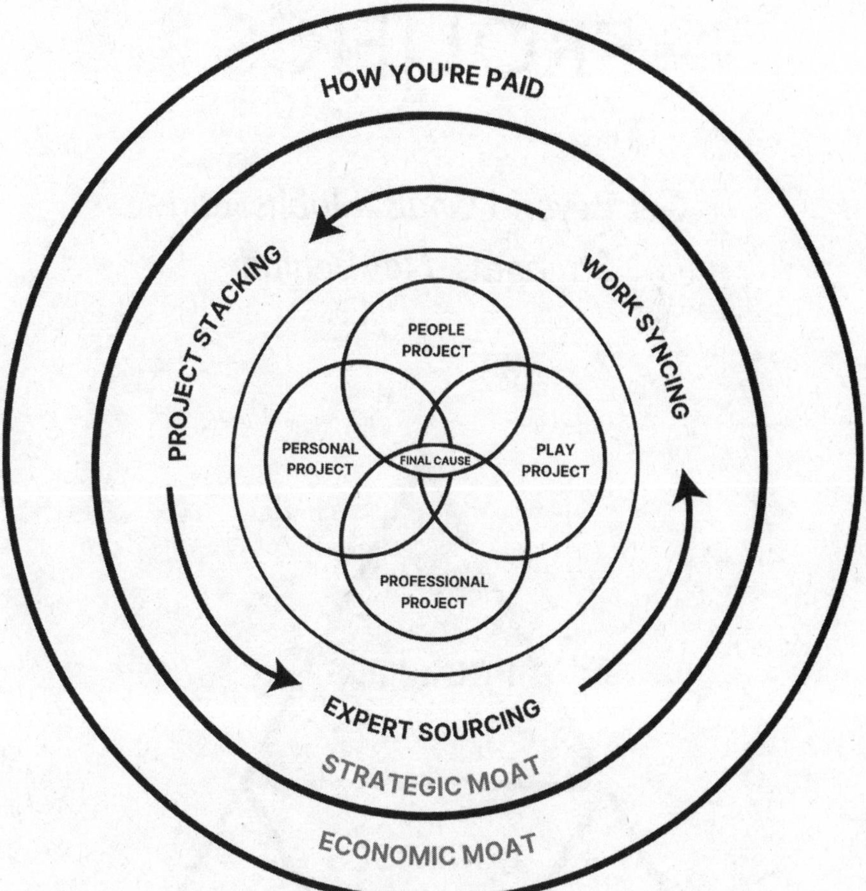
HOW YOU'RE PAID
PROJECT STACKING
WORK SYNCING
PEOPLE PROJECT
PERSONAL PROJECT
FINAL CAUSE
PLAY PROJECT
PROFESSIONAL PROJECT
EXPERT SOURCING
STRATEGIC MOAT
ECONOMIC MOAT

PART IV
PROLIFICS

Get Beyond Goals, Habits, and Strengths, Not Behind

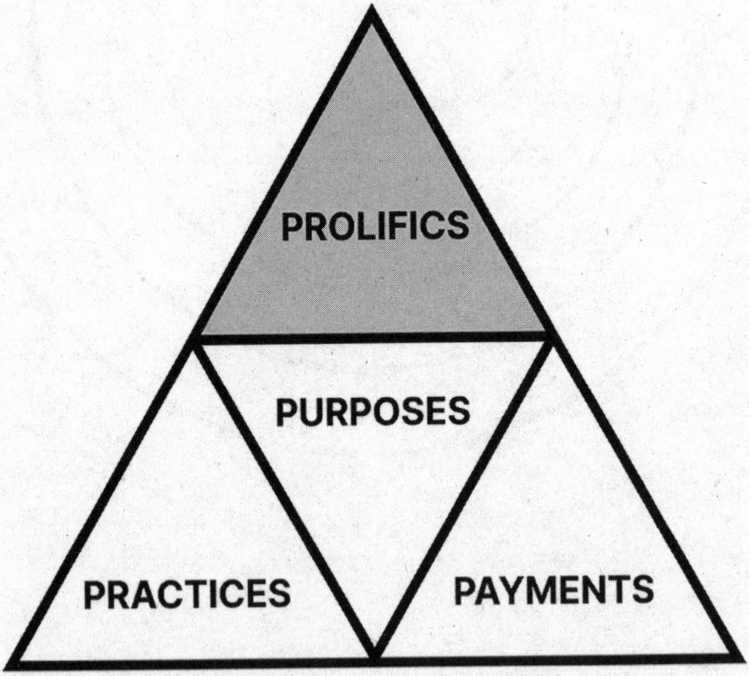

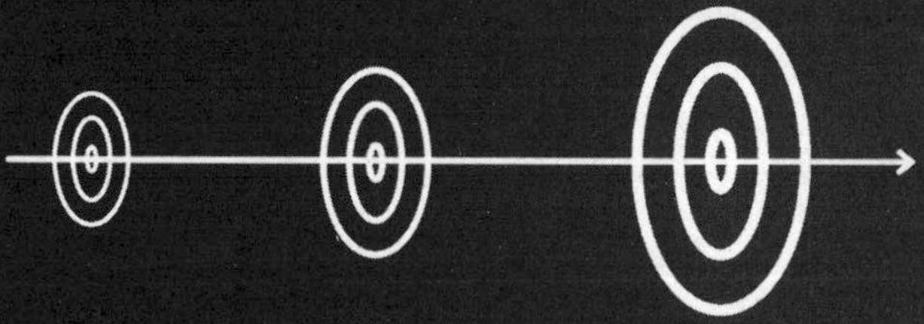

GET BEYOND GOALS, HABITS, AND STRENGTHS, NOT BEHIND.

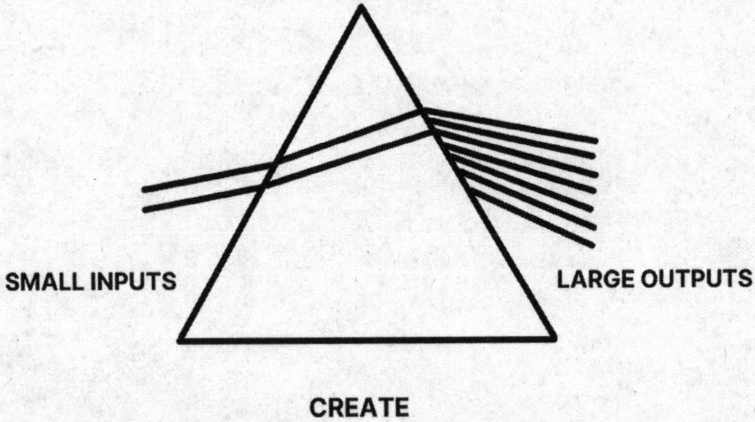

PRISMIC PRODUCTIVITY

CHAPTER 9

Create Prismic Productivity

How to Choose Small Inputs That Create an Array of Big Results

> My mission in life is not merely to survive, but to thrive; and to do so with some passion, some compassion, some humor, and some style.
>
> —MAYA ANGELOU

Bryce and Nellie Jurgensmeier traveled with our family on the road for a few months when our kids were little—from the Rocky Mountains of Utah to the beaches of Mexico, to the scenic views of Canada and back.

It happened on a whim.

I heard Bryce speak at an event, and later we met. Bryce was trying to negotiate how to leave his job. Nellie wanted to stay in her job. Their dream was to travel and make money on the road like we were doing. They dreamed that one day, when they had kids, they could take them on adventures on the road.

Natalie and I told them we'd be happy to show them how we do it and invited them on the road with us. Along the way we shared ideas with Bryce on how he could leave his job while maintaining good relations with his boss. He did. We also shared ideas with Nellie on how to do her work remotely. She did. We had a ton of fun, made money, and created new opportunities along the way.

Bryce says:

> Meeting you and having one conversation helped me realize I did know trades and principles that could make others a lot of money, and you instilled in me the confidence to offer that. "Change your question, change your life."
>
> Now, five years later from when we first started implementing, what began as a road trip on YouTube has now led to us owning and running an RV park outside of Yellowstone! What?! And we make content to promote that while building it, so we're double- and triple-dipping during the hours we work to then not work when we're together at the times we want.
>
> It's too foreign to me to now go back to a schedule that a job controls. We control our schedule—we can still definitely improve—but this life is way better. I remember feeling so awkward to charge someone $1,000 for something, and now we're about to sign a contract for $200,000 with a company!

Today, they are full-time RV living with their two little girls.

The Jurgys are incredible examples to me of what *Prismic Productivity* looks like—small inputs creating large outputs.

I hope you take from this story the fact that they did all the work to make it happen. All the ideas, books, coaches, videos, mentors, and advice you get are worth zero without action.

Prismic Productivity means sharing your results with others and helping them do the same. Your life and work and business can't depend on a fixed mindset. You must have a growth mindset to expand your opportunities and contribute to the best of your ability—*and be a change catalyst by sharing with others how to do it too along the way.*

Tip your time and inspire others to *Time Tip* too.

Choose Your Map

California was known as an island for centuries.

I'm not surprised. I met a teen who told me Alaska was an island near Hawaii. I was confused until I looked at a map and saw Alaska clearly placed next to Hawaii as an island.

If you're in China, you'll see the map of the world with China in the middle. If you are in Europe, you'll find the world's map with Europe in the middle. We see, behave, and interact with the world largely like we see and interpret maps.

The compasses we use are only as good as the maps we're trying to follow.

Better have the right map!

We live at the center of our own map. Your map has helped you make the decisions that have gotten you to where you are today—detours and all. Moving forward requires assessing where you're at, finding out if you're on course, and reorienting your life in the direction you want to go. It's good to rethink, but rethinking is futile if you're rethinking routes on the wrong map.

You won't get far if your compass is pointing at yourself.

Time Tippers look in and reach out.

In the musical *The King and I,* British schoolteacher Anna breaks into song—"Getting to Know You"—with the children of Siam just after showing them a new map. The modern map shows a tiny Siam. Trying to relate with the children so different from her, Anna points out that England is even smaller. However, after the song and dance are over, the children dramatically claim their disbelief, exclaiming, "Siam not so small!" Their identity had been challenged (and changed) by a new map.

Your self-identity can shift without realizing it, but a new map of the way you see the world will make you question it all. Autonomy can challenge your identity when you haven't had it. When you produce greater time and money with your energy, you're opening new maps. New environments and new ways of doing things inherently come along with adventure and change. *Time Tippers* do things using a treasure map of time. Only, the *X* that marks the spot is where you're standing, right now—not in some distant land.

There are other ways to see the world than with maps. Many programs and gurus will show you kaleidoscopes of ideas—often distorting the world from reality to fantasy.

Time Tippers clarify their worldview and energy through the lens of *Prismic Productivity*—turning the way you see the world into a prism of positive possibility.

Measure your life for great impact by honoring the little time you have by making small things create big results.

Make the Small World Smaller and the Universe Bigger

Prismic Productivity *happens when small inputs create large outputs.* Prismic Productivity is laser-focused work on time-centered, results-oriented activities unlocking an array of asymmetrical, varied opportunities—*the crescendo of Time Tipping.*

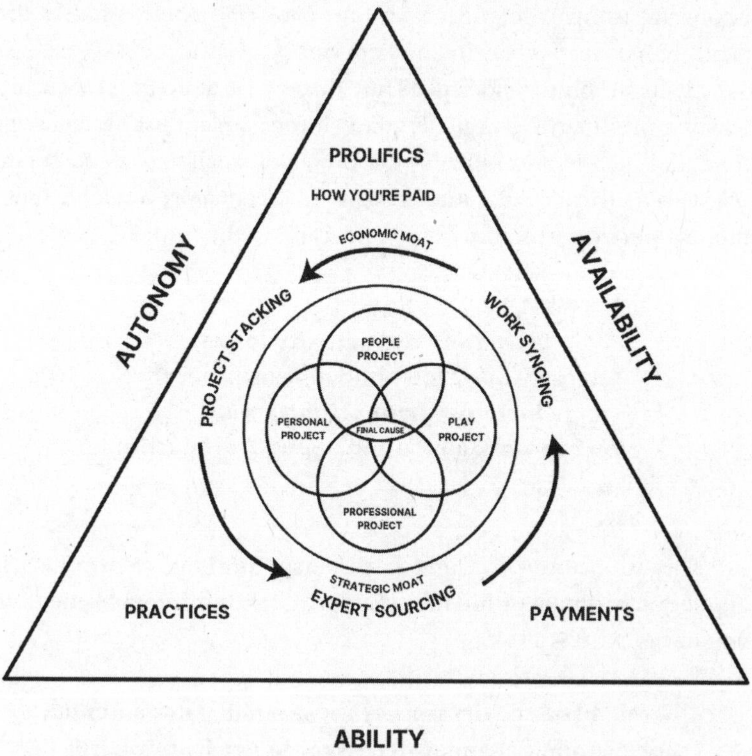

The *Time Tipping Framework* is the prism by which tiny inputs bend to create giant outputs. Prismic Productivity is how super-productive people do a lot of different things with time to spare. In a prism, a single white light entering on one side will refract into a colorful array on the other.

Prismic Productivity is the way to get off the hamster wheel but keep it spinning. I received this message from an executive coach: "I'm on a giant hamster wheel about to leap off and run free, but at the last minute [I keep] getting nervous or something comes up and [I] just stay on the wheel." Many people have a similar feeling—like they're always spinning but never moving forward with no way out.

When you realize how fragile life is, you want to make the small things that matter count big time. A *prismic mindset* has been important to my wife and me in our *Time Tipping* efforts after the death of her brother Gavin and later our son Gavin.

"Time-in" on the clock does not always have a direct relationship to your productive output. Finding inverse relationships between time and money and utilizing the power of small actions to create big, asymmetrical results is an art that can create more available time, money, and opportunities for you now and in the future.

Increasing opportunity losses.
You can work a lot without being productive.
Increasing opportunity wins.
You can work a little and be super-productive.

This isn't about working hard versus working smart. This is about measuring your life for great impact, honoring the little time you have.

Prismic Productivity refines those small, fundamental, overlooked changes necessary to get from where you are to where you want to be.

Make Money and Meaning with Prismic Productivity

Time Tipping teaches you to make decisions from *purpose* that fall into three parts to generate Prismic Productivity: *priorities, practices, and payments*—the castle, the Strategic Moat, and the Economic Moat.

Reclaiming your time and revolutionizing your results is accelerated and expanded through Prismic Productivity—the synthesis of *Time Tipping*. World-class high achievers begin mentally from (1) where they want to be, (2) create an atmosphere where they can practice living that way, and (3) create a way to get paid based on their values and the value they create to grow with this way of life as it expands.

The children's book author. Eevi Jones once wanted to write a children's book. So she did. Then she wanted to help others write their own magical story. So she did. And then she felt called to write children's books with and for those she admired. So again, she did.

Eevi is a German Vietnamese *USA Today* and *Wall Street Journal* bestselling and award-winning author living near DC with her husband and two boys. She says some of the most powerful concepts that she has followed throughout her writing career have helped her get to where she is. Today she is taking action, having courage, and avoiding regrets.

She says:

> Moving away from distractions and instead focusing on taking action toward these goals of mine, I now have written, co-authored, and ghostwritten more than fifty children's books. And during the writing of these books, I've come to understand what being courageous means. To me, it takes courage to be confident. And it takes confidence to show courage.
>
> If you're anything like me, you too might worry about being rejected or about failing whenever you're trying something new. In one of my children's books, I wrote: "The worst you can feel is the weight of regret of not having taken any action just yet. Taking action weighs ounces, regret weighs a ton. So, 10 years from now, what will you wish you had done?" Reminding myself that I don't want to feel regret later on in life always motivates me to take action—that first step toward my goals.
>
> So in order to be able to spend more time with my family, I knew I simply had to take action and focus on the essentials of my business only. And with the help of a little bit of courage and the unwillingness to experience regret down the road, I was able to move beyond distractions and instead focus on taking action toward my goals, one step at a time.

The guy who makes things happen. Ramon Ray was working at the United Nations for more than ten years. It was a well-paying job and financially took care of his family. However, he had a yearning for something more. At the time, he wasn't sure what that would look like. But he knew he loved changing the rules and coloring outside the lines. Eventually, he was fired and was thrust into full-time entrepreneurship.

Ramon said, "All of this dreaming and doing can take a toll on a person. While we try to move forward optimistically, we also torment ourselves by focusing on past mistakes, the things we haven't achieved, and the comparison of where we are versus where we thought we'd be by now." Truly, life is crazy.

Ramon has now started four companies and sold two of them—"neat little companies," as he calls them, that he's been passionate about. He's built a steady flow of large-brand clients in the tech industry who seek him out to speak at their events and produce content for them. He worked hard and prioritized that work in a way that is fulfilling.

He says, "I've been able to have days free to spend with family, friends. I'm able to join my church on multiday projects to serve others in need. I'm able to experiment and play with new projects." In fact, he's been invited to the White House, shared the stage with celebrities, interviewed the president of the United States, and interviewed all five sharks from *Shark Tank*.

Feel the Mental Clarity of the Overview Effect

When astronauts go into outer space, they don't just see the world differently, they get clarity.

> On July 16, 1969, the day of the launch, the Apollo 11 crew became some of the first people to look down at Earth from space. Aldrin called it "a brilliant jewel in the black velvet sky." This state of mental clarity, called the "overview effect," occurs when you are flung so far away from Earth that you become totally overwhelmed and awed by the fragility and unity of life on our blue globe. It's the uncanny sense of understanding

the "big picture," and of feeling connected to and yet bigger than the intricate processes bubbling on Earth.

Your expansive universe begins with your head above the clouds.

David Beaver, co-founder of the Overview Institute, recounts the sentiments from one of the astronauts on the Apollo 8 mission: "When we originally went to the moon, our total focus was on the moon. We weren't thinking about looking back at the Earth. But now that we've done it, that may well have been the most important reason we went." Author and philosopher David Loy said, "It was quite a shock; I don't think any of us had any expectations about how it would give us such a different perspective. I think the focus had been: we're going to the stars, we're going to other planets. . . . And suddenly we look back at ourselves and it seems to imply a new kind of self-awareness."

Giving space to things also puts them into focus.

One of the more common words used to describe Earth from space is *fragile.*

Your world is fragile.

A whole new map. Like explorers, astronauts live in the adventure of new maps that redefine the way we see the world. In the process, those who dare to explore the unknown also redefine themselves—*and the rest of us.* But is a new map what explorers are really looking for? Or is mapmaking a work project that helps them achieve their personal dreams through quests of Final Cause?

Blending work-life dreams is the mark of great parents, inventors, artists, creatives, explorers, entrepreneurs, professionals, athletes, scientists, and on and on—like a continuum of positive change.

Prioritize Attention to Priorities

Time Tippers see the world differently and redefine maps to put the *things that matter most* clearly into perspective. The times and seasons give us time and reason to make meaning wherever we are on the map. Syncing your attention and daily rhythm to *purpose-centered priorities* keeps your activities and time aligned *despite distraction.*

- » **Attention synchronization** in *Time Tipping* dynamically processes your relevant time demands for flexibility and efficiency of your goals.
- » **Rhythmic synchronization** in *Time Tipping* extracts patterns from your life and moves your activities' relationship to your available time based on anticipation.

Keeping your work and home priorities in rhythm with no regrets is a matter of attention.

Time flexibility depends on your selection of priorities.

Creating more time for more things becomes less relevant when what you're doing is what you already want to do.

Identify the Productivity Paradox in Your Life

THE PRODUCTIVITY PARADOX

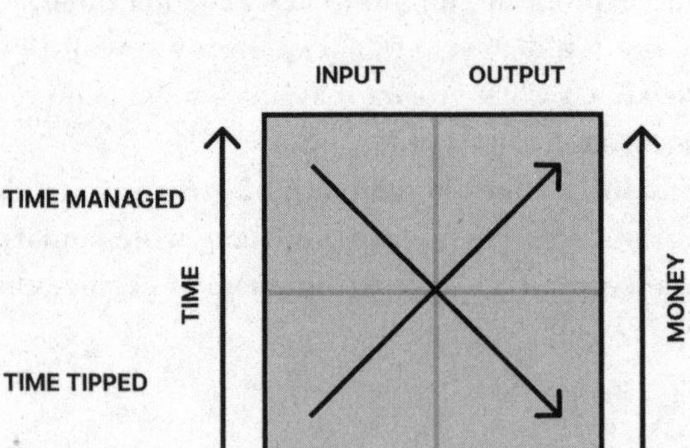

I call this the *Productivity Paradox*: *small inputs can create large outputs, while large inputs can create small outputs* (positive or negative asymmetrical results).

Prismic Productivity happens when small inputs create large outputs.

Prismic Productivity, through the *Time Tipping Framework*, means one decision turns into many happy results—an array of new life and work options. The energy you put into making money and the amount of money that is generated are not equal to each other.

Since *Time Tippers* are not gambling with time and results, they find a way to mitigate risk through testing their ideas in the present. *Time Tippers* put their time and energy into results they want by both *living the would-be benefits of those results the best they can now* and *creating work that serves this purpose before even accomplishing the end goal.*

Through *Time Tipped* alignment, you can receive, process, and share information about what works and what doesn't—living the life you want in bold discovery. Independence is only as independent as the people and processes you can trust.

Priorities, Pitfalls, Proliferation, Procrastination, Perfection

At the beginning of our marriage, Natalie and I set an intention. She wrote about it on her blog years ago:

> We've worked so hard, Richie and I, to set up our lives intentionally. Early in our marriage, we sat down together and decided upon staunch priorities surrounding what we wanted our life together to look and feel like. (NOTE: It's no surprise that the majority of those goals centered around the kind of life we hoped to be able to provide for our children.)

I'm so happy to report (to myself more than anyone else) that despite pitfalls, roadblocks, discouragement, and outright failures (yes, plural), we've remained committed to the things we deemed (together) to matter the very most. Case in point is the ability to drive the boys to school together in the mornings and the luxury of picking them up together in the afternoons.

This is a small example of a bigger-picture reality we have worked so hard to achieve. Not to say that we've got it all perfect. We still have SO (so so so so so SO) far to go, but we're on the right path—the pathway toward our intentional life, and it is so absolutely energizing and fulfilling that my heart nearly bursts with joy just thinking about it.

Intentional living will look different for everyone, but friends, do the work to get clear (about what you want your life to look like) and then get busy (creating the life of your dreams). You CAN do it, and you'll be so glad you did! Allow me to leave you with one of my favorite quotes from Ms. Karen Lamb: "A year from now, you'll wish you started today."

When you decide who you want to be, you'll know what to do.

If we want to sincerely enjoy our lives, who we become along the way is far more important than what we achieve.

You and I aren't perfect. We never will be.

So you and I will do what we can, here and now.

Proliferation produces perfection better than procrastination.

Gaining even small amounts of time for your priorities (and prioritizing how you spend that time), despite pitfalls, is a major win with snowball momentum and revolutionary implications.

» If you can gain an hour today, what's to say you can't also gain an hour tomorrow? A whole month off? A year? Two years of total autonomy?

» A lifetime of choices and goals lived over the next two to five to ten years?

» What if it only takes a few months or weeks?

Sometimes what you *actually* want to do *is the responsible thing* to do. Don't shortchange your family and yourself.

Don't leave your free time unloved like a wrapped gift.

The key to personal growth and happiness is knowing the difference between planning for the future and sabotaging the present.

Strategize *prismic success.*

Choose Both Money and Meaning for Prismic Productivity

One of the biggest small inputs that creates the biggest results is to choose both money and meaning as you move through professional projects.

This is the Money Versus Meaning Matrix I created to help me decide which projects to take on. I've also found this matrix to be incredibly helpful when working with clients. In fact, this tool has turned struggling entrepreneurs and organizations around in mission and in income—so much so that some of the largest sales teams for various projects have been built around this tool to help people be successful and customize their work to their aspirations.

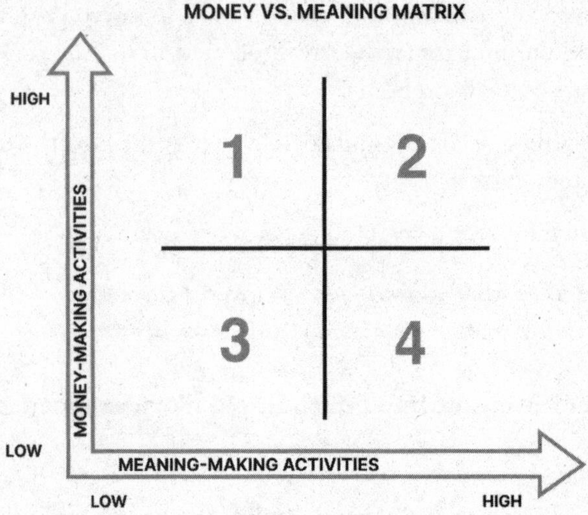

Quadrant 1: This is where you make a lot of money, but the work is not really meaningful to you. You're happy you're prospering, sure, but you find you burn out easily (or get bored, or both), and you wish you were getting more deep satisfaction out of your work/life. From the outside looking in, it would appear that you've got it all, but there is definitely something missing on the inside. You long to use your talents and passions to make a meaningful contribution in your industry (or another one altogether), but unfortunately, you're just too busy making money.

Quadrant 2: In Quadrant 2, you're making money while simultaneously experiencing real satisfaction from the meaningful work in which you're engaged. You're happy to be living a comfortable and sustainable lifestyle, your work fulfills you, *and* you're deeply satisfied by the contribution you're making in your industry/the world. Quadrant 2, my friends, is the sweet spot.

Quadrant 3: This is where you seem to be struggling to make ends meet constantly. The income just doesn't ever seem to be enough for you to experience real, sustainable financial security—let alone ever get ahead. Furthermore, the work you're doing seems meaningless.

You may feel trapped, and you definitely find yourself wishing that things were very different. At times, you may even feel hopeless. You find yourself desperately waiting for either circumstances to magically change or an opportunity to come along for you to do something different.

Quadrant 4: This is where the work you're doing is fulfilling and making a meaningful difference. You love what you do. The work fuels and excites you. But as it stands, the work is simply not making enough money to be sustainable. You may find yourself resenting money, overwhelmed and discouraged by the need to bring in consistent cash flow when all you want to do is make a difference in the world. You would give anything to be able to stop worrying about when, where, or how the next paycheck will arrive and whether it will be enough to keep things afloat. Meaningful work is great, but if you're in Quadrant 4 and it's not profitable, you likely feel a considerable amount of inner conflict or "mission drift," because no matter how meaningful the work you're doing actually is, you still have to be able to pay the bills.

CREATE PRISMIC PRODUCTIVITY

Prismic Productivity is about becoming the best version of yourself and having the time to enjoy it and help others even when circumstances overwhelm.

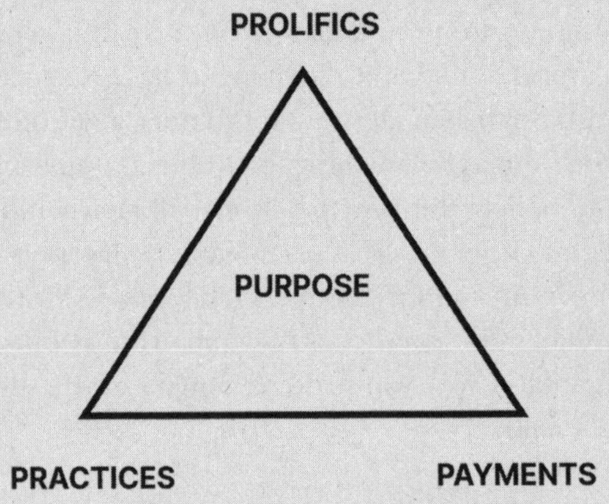

Part 1: Answer the following questions.

1. Are my choices and activities leading me closer to or further away from my highest priorities (the Four-*Ps*)?
2. If my choices move me closer to my goals, how can I realize these goals through the *Time Tipping Framework*?
3. If my choices are not bringing me closer to my priorities, do I need to change my choices and daily activities, or do I need to change my priorities?

The Four-*Ps* become the most important things in your life. Think of them as your North Star. The Four-*Ps* in the *Time Tipping Framework* are the prism to filter your opportunities.

Part 2: Answer the following questions.

The Money-Meaning Matrix

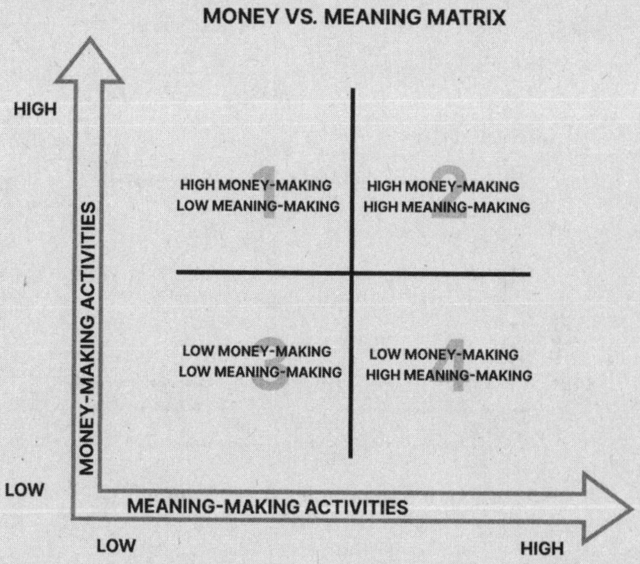

The Money Versus Meaning Matrix, in a nutshell:

1. Plot your life priorities and goals currently where they fit to optimize your *Final Cause Projects* and *How You Get Paid* for Quadrant 2.

Quadrant 1: This is where you make a lot of money, but the work is not meaningful to you.

Quadrant: 2: This is where you're making money while simultaneously experiencing real satisfaction from the meaningful work and life in which you're engaged.

Quadrant 3: This is where you seem to be constantly struggling to make ends meet.

Quadrant 4: This is where the work you're doing is fulfilling and making a meaningful difference, but it's not financially sustainable and you're experiencing mission drift.

So, where do you fit in?

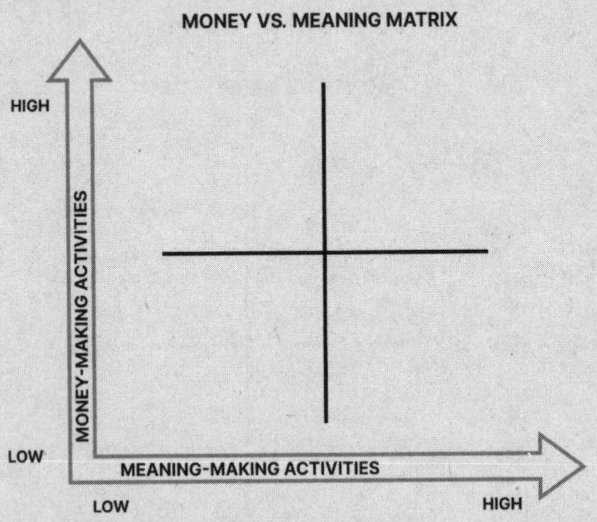

2. Plot your current situation, then ask yourself:

—Why am I here? How can I move from where I am to where I want to be?

—Am I willing to make the sacrifice to get there (or stay there)?

—What one thing can I do today to move myself closer to Quadrant 2?

3. Align your *Final Cause Projects* and *How You Get Paid* with Quadrant 2 to identify what laser-like activities to focus on to create *Prismic Productivity* for greater meaning in life.

Focus on creating proper business models around your Four-*Ps Final Cause Projects* to create a meaningful lifestyle that is also financially sustainable.

Get Your Free Download of the Money Versus Meaning Worksheet and Other Anti-Time Management Tools at RichieNorton.com/Time.

ASK BETTER QUESTIONS, GET BETTER ANSWERS.

CHAPTER 10

Ask Better Questions, Get Better Answers

How to Quickly Upgrade Your Thoughts

Never lose a holy curiosity.
—ALBERT EINSTEIN

Several months before Albert Einstein's death, a young man (a freshman at Harvard) visited Einstein in his small home without an appointment and asked, "Does experience give us truth?"

Einstein responded, "This is a difficult question. One is always seeing things without being sure that one does see them. Truth is a verbal concept, which cannot be submitted to mathematical proof."

Einstein "was wearing sandals, baggy slacks and a gray woolen pullover sweater, a tieless shirt open at the neck [and] . . . the lucid windows of his eyes seemed to reveal not a man but an embodiment of pure thought."

After some conversation, Einstein gave this profound advice. "A child with great intuition could not grow up to become something worthwhile in life without some knowledge. However, there comes a point in everyone's life where only intuition can make the leap ahead, without knowing precisely how."

Professor Hermanns, a longtime friend from Germany who had "volunteered for World War I, lived through the indescribable carnage of the Battle of Verdun, been captured and imprisoned for three years by the French . . . then a fugitive from Hitler," prompted Einstein and said, "You do believe in a soul."

Einstein replied, "Yes, if by this you mean the living spirit that makes us long to do worthy things for humanity."

Einstein turned to the student and said, "Does not the question of the undulation of light arouse your curiosity?" (The student's father later commented, "The nicest thing about the question was his simple assumption that the boy would understand it.")

Einstein further questioned, "Is not this enough to occupy your whole curiosity for a lifetime?"

The student replied, "Why, yes. I guess it is."

Then these questions prompted one of the most beautiful and profound statements.

"Then do not stop to think about the reasons for what you are doing, about why you are questioning. The important thing is not to stop questioning. Curiosity has its own reason for existence," Einstein shared.

"One cannot help but be in awe when he contemplates the mysteries of eternity, of life, of the marvelous structure of reality. It is enough if one tries merely to comprehend a little of this mystery each day. Never lose a holy curiosity. Try not to become a man of success but rather try to become a man of value. He is considered successful in our day who gets more out of life than he puts in. But a man of value will give more than he receives."

In parting, the student pointed to a tree in Einstein's yard and asked "whether one could truthfully say it was a tree."

Einstein said, "This could all be a dream. You may not be seeing it at all."

The student replied, "If I assume that I can see it, how do I know exactly that the tree exists and where it is?"

Einstein then imparted this wisdom: "You have to assume something. Be glad that you have some little knowledge of something that you cannot penetrate. Don't stop to marvel."

Not every question has an answer, but every question can keep you curious.

Do you want to stay open to learning, doing, and knowing new things you haven't experienced yet? Experience isn't everything in creating—intuition, assumptions, and a little extra knowledge help you make the leap when you don't know exactly what to do.

The traditional ladder climb keeps people from asking questions and reaching for dreams outside their limited experience. Ladder climbers shy away from looking for answers outside their laddered experience for fear of being wrong or appearing naive.

When you don't know what you're seeing, keep asking questions. Be curious. *Don't stop to marvel.*

Stop setting goals from your experience.

Goals inside experience are tasks. Goals outside experience are growth.

Ask Better Questions

"We were in about $50,000 of medical debt because my wife, Katie, was diagnosed with multiple sclerosis several years prior," said Shawn Van Dyke.

> My job as an executive at a construction company wasn't cutting it. Plus, I was working sixty to seventy hours a week, never present with our family of seven, and stressed out all the time. I needed a new way to make more money, one that didn't require me to be in the office or on the construction site. I needed more flexibility in my schedule so I could care for my wife. But most of all I wanted to travel with my wife and my family and have adventures with our family before my wife was physically unable to do so.

I asked Shawn what his plans were over the next two years. He had big goals, but after he told me he thought he needed to first build an audience and blog for two years before selling something, I decided I should ask him a different question, "What if you could hit your goals in the next four to six months?"

Shawn said, "Could I?"

No one could know for sure, of course. But we reasoned that the same person who discovers him two years from now isn't that much different from the person discovering him now if they didn't follow his blog for two years.

"Why wait when you're ready now?"

With that question in mind, Shawn went to work and found ways to accelerate the "get to know you" process and began selling—making money within his first two weeks, the same money that he thought would take two years.

Fast-forward five years, and Shawn says, "I have become a top-rated author, a nationally recognized keynote speaker, and have launched a business training and coaching academy for contractors. I can now work when I choose. I can travel with my family, and my business runs itself. I work half as much as I used to, and I have quadrupled my income." In fact, Shawn was awarded IKON Entrepreneur of the Year.

Learning to ask the right questions of ourselves allows us to jump learning curves. Questions ignited Shawn's curiosity and changed how he approached his time and life. His goals and achievements have expanded far beyond that original conversation. In this way, you can transition between roles and create hybrid solutions.

Different Questions Create Different Lives

A mentor of mine said, "Ask better questions, get better answers." It was an off-the-cuff statement, but I took it to heart and have practically made a science of it.

Neal Hooper had a steady paycheck working with a Fortune 100 company but was miserable. He asked himself how he could make his priorities a priority. That simple question changed the trajectory of his life. He said, "I was at a fork in the road of my life, but now I have passion, purpose, and I have the lifestyle and time to prioritize what's most important."

Jan Oshiro was faced with a dilemma when her husband, at fifty-two years of age, was going through a disability and being turned down for long-term care insurance. With her husband's disability, Jan was unsure of how to pay for long-term care should he need it, and her rental portfolio had gone negative since the rental market had tanked. She was a general manager of a freight company and was consumed with "fixing" a broken company. She was inundated with daily issues, conflicts, and lack of revenue.

She asked herself how she could make some money on the side.

Jan says, "I had started a hobby creating and selling healing gemstone jewelry. I created systems to free my time to enjoy my hobby business, travel more, and invest in assets that would eventually provide financial freedom when I retire. I achieved that at sixty-five years old and will be retiring at sixty-six years. The beauty of this is I am working because I love to work, not because I need to. Being financially free gave me a new perspective on how a person should structure their life. It's wonderful living a life free of financial worries."

She advises, "Keep your eyes and ears open for opportunities to serve the community. Focus on your full-time job with the key elements of *Time Tipping* until the part-time hobbies exceed your pay from your full-time job. Then employ the full force of *Time Tipping*, and your path will open and explode."

Steve and Gail Halladay started a small business selling pumice stones for toilet cleaning on Amazon. They researched the competition, read the Amazon reviews, saw what people were complaining about, worked with a supplier to make a better product, and then placed the first order. They said, "We invested a few thousand dollars for the first shipment, and that's it. We never financed anything, just kept growing by reinvesting profits. Fast-forward five or six years, and we beat all the competition on Amazon, including the market leader who's been in business for seventy-five years; we now have close to nineteen thousand reviews with a 4.6 star rating (people are passionate about having clean toilets). We just sold our business for close to $2 million, from an initial $3,000 investment. Not bad." Not bad at all.

Sean McLellan was raised by his grandparents in a decades-old camper while they spent a decade building their dream home by hand—an 1800s-style hand-hewn log home, one log at a time. Sean says, "We had no money at all. Almost less than no money." Sean grew up, got married to Mel, moved, and started his own life.

At one point he asked himself, "If earning money didn't matter, what would things be like?" He says, "I came home and asked my wife the same question. What would life look like on a day-to-day basis if we didn't need to earn money? Her answer was almost identical to mine: find land, live closer to my grandparents, have a garden. What on earth were we doing, then? Why not just figure out how to do what we eventually wanted . . . right now?"

Within three months they found a house with land next door to his grandparents and moved in. Eventually, Sean and Mel created a business that involved their kids and his grandparents. They made enough money to get completely out of debt. Paid off their house and bought their grandparents' house from them and let them live there rent-free. They ultimately sold the business.

Sean says:

> We are having a great time together as a family. I'm spending more time with my beautiful wife and our kids and my grandmother, now. Unfortunately, my grandfather completely unexpectedly passed away at the end of last year. So it turns out that moving next door and starting up all the changes that we did over the past decade was even more the exact right move than we thought it was. As hard as losing him has been, I can't imagine how much harder it would be if I had to live with the regret of our kids not being close to him and us not having lived next door to each other and having spent the time building the business that we did together. And now we're making the most of life.

Your Questions Are the Precursor to Your Future

Consider these questions. What's the first thing that pops into your mind?

» Are you waiting to have more money so you can have more time?

» Right now, is most of your time going to your Final Cause priorities or not?

» Are your family and friends taking a backseat to your work?

Asking "better" questions may create an intentionally uncomfortable gap between what you want and how you'll get there.

Begin with Final Cause Questions

When you're solving for the success after the success—most problems can be approached with an abundance of space for various possible answers. In that sense, approach the success you want for the sake of what matters most (instead of following an erroneous map that a time manager created for their own purposes), like the overview effect from space looking at your world with more delicacy and appreciation. Consciously ask questions from Final Cause about what you would do if you were already in that position to enter the *Time Tipping* atmosphere.

Prevent Fires

Our refrigerator caught fire. We quickly unplugged the refrigerator, and it stopped burning. It turns out it was an electrical problem caused by water dripping from a faulty water filter. There was a light on telling us to change the filter—we just didn't do anything about it.

So, why did the refrigerator catch fire? Looking back, was it an electrical issue, a filter issue, or user error? Depending on the question, goal, and bias, all those answers are correct.

» Looking backward creates historical footnotes dependent on the point of view of what's relevant and impacts how I will spend my time now on the problem.

» Looking forward generates different questions and directions in how I will spend my time now on the problem.

What happens with how my time is spent if I ask a forward-looking question like this: *"Where are we going to buy a new refrigerator?"*

When you push questions through the thought filter of time, you generate a variety of new questions to discern better answers related to your time purposes.

How does the nature of your questions impact how you spend your time?

When problem-solving, ask yourself what questions you should ask to create more time while solving the problem in a sustainable way with the most upside (and the least amount of downside).

Putting out the little fires with *Time Tipped questions* can help you put out big fires *before they happen.*

Considering various points of view changes behavior.

There are little fires in our lives almost every day—as you put them out, see them as a way to refine your process and change the way things are done so you can eliminate, delegate, and outsource the things that negatively impact your time.

Ask Yourself These Seven *Time Tipping* Questions

Take personal inventory. A year or two from now, what do you think you want your ideal life to look like to feel fulfilled?

1. **Final Cause:** What does success look like for you after the goal?
2. **Meta-Decisions:** But what will you *really* prioritize, and who do you want to become in the process?

3. **Meta-Projects:** What project(s) can you start to fulfill your big-picture purposes?
4. **Project Stacking:** What overlap is there between your projects so one priority can meet the goals of many purposes at the same time?
5. **Work Syncing:** What would your aligned work-life practices look like if your projects could happen without you?
6. **Expert Sourcing:** Who can do this for you (or with you)?
7. **Payment Orientation:** What ways can you get paid that support you living your principles, dreams, and values (Final Cause) easier, right now?

What if your vision of the next year or two could happen in the next six months or less? What will you begin now to make that happen? What needs to happen for you to create an environment where you act from your future instead of from your past?

What do you think your happiest life looks like?

Make It Urgent and Important

By leveraging existing resources and acting from the future you want to live, instead of toward it, you create a *prismic effect* of many expected and unexpected possibilities.

Here are questions to help you make *Time Tipping* happen sooner than later:

- What will make this urgent for me?
- What stopped me in the past from doing this?
- What if I overcame all my excuses?

Asking "*What would I do if I knew how to do it?*" versus "*What would I do if I hired someone who knew how to do it?*" versus "*What would I do if this could earn money without taking away my time?*" can create very different futures.

Align Questions with Purpose with Priorities with Projects with Payments

Don't cheat yourself. Too often people are scared to ask what they really want for fear of its not being possible or any host of nonsensical reasons to stay put. Instead, align your questions with the success you want after the goal is achieved and watch a host of nonsensical excuses disappear as the answers emerge.

Better Questions ← → Purpose ← → Priorities ← → Projects ← → Payments

You Don't Have to Quit Your Job

John Mashni was swamped with work at his law practice. "I wanted to spend more time with my wife, kids, and family. I wanted to build something that allowed me to make money without sacrificing the best parts of my life," he said. "I wanted to write. I wanted to create a business that allowed me to take control of my time."

He learned to embrace the idea that others would think his new ideas were crazy because *the goal beyond the goal was bigger than the fear of change.* He began asking himself what he could do to better embody his values in daily living. Then he decided to dive into his passion of writing children's books—an unlikely decision from anyone looking in from the outside.

John said, "I had a busy law practice, and writing a silly children's book was not the move anyone around me anticipated. But it was the right one. I now spend more time with my kids, and we have so much fun writing and working on books that bring joy to kids and parents. Plus, when you introduced me to the concept of *Time Tipping*, you inspired me to build a law practice that fit my skills and goals rather than one that just made other people wealthy. I learned to stop waiting to live."

Time Tippers don't have to quit their jobs or end something that pays the bills (if they don't want to). You can make room for your priorities and projects by asking better questions that impact both your professional and your personal life for greater *ability*, *availability*, and *autonomy* to make meaning.

"I needed to stop thinking that life will be better in five years or ten years or whenever," John said. "I needed to start living the exact life that I want to live today instead of thinking that my perfect life was far away. Life is short. You never know when your time will come. In a world where there are lots of people peddling advice, *Time Tipping* spreads sprinkles of wisdom for people who are paying attention, like I am now. My life will never be the same."

Questions beget questions, but aligned questions support inspired action.

Ask Questions That Can Change Everything

Consider these three legendary questions and apply them to your own situation:

> ***"Life's most persistent and urgent question is, 'What are you doing for others?'"***

Martin Luther King Jr. said, "Every person must decide at some point whether they will walk in the light of creative altruism or in the darkness of destructive selfishness. This is the judgment: 'Life's most persistent and urgent question is, what are you doing for others?'"

> ***"If today were the last day of my life, would I want to do what I'm about to do today?"***

Steve Jobs said, "When I was 17, I read a quote that went something like: 'If you live each day as if it was your last, someday you'll most certainly be right.' It made an impression on me, and since then, for the past 33 years, I have looked in the mirror every morning and asked myself: 'If today were the last day of my life, would I want to do what I am about to do today?' And whenever the answer has been 'no' for too many days in a row, I know I need to change something."

"What, if anything, about the way people are leading today needs to change?"

Brené Brown asked, "What, if anything, about the way people are leading today needs to change in order for leaders to be successful in a complex, rapidly changing environment where we're faced with seemingly intractable challenges and an insatiable demand for innovation?"

What question haven't you asked yourself?

Be Discerning

I predict discernment will become the number-one leadership competency of this century. Leaders, entrepreneurs, and individuals who learn to discern will have the unique and rare advantage to help more people, add more value, and create better experiences for those they care for, love, and serve.

Discernment comes from asking better questions. For leaders, entrepreneurs, creatives, businesspersons, and individual decision makers, the skill of discernment allows you to see more than one opportunity and more than one perspective as well as avoid the law of increasing opportunity costs.

Direction. Charles Dickens may have described the multidimensional, asynchronous nature of truths and the essence of discernment best in *A Tale of Two Cities* when he said, "It was the best of times, it was the worst of times, it was the age of wisdom, it was the age of foolishness, it was the epoch of belief, it was the epoch of incredulity, it was the season of Light, it was the season of Darkness, it was the spring of hope, it was the winter of despair, we had everything before us, we had nothing before us, we were all going direct to Heaven, we were all going direct the other way." Today, you're facing both the best and worst of humanity.

What's the best way to move forward? Begin with Final Cause. Your job as a *Time Tipper* is to discern by asking better questions so you can find the answers on the best map out there and navigate your life and work in a way that leads you closer and closer to your big-picture dreams (the Four-*P*s) as you live for the sake of them in your everyday life.

Why are you asking $1 questions when with the same breath you could be asking $1 million questions?

Change your questions, change your life.

Welcome to your future. Now that you've freed your time, how will you spend it? More importantly, who will you become in the process?

EXAMPLE CHAPTER ACTIVITY: BETTER QUESTIONS

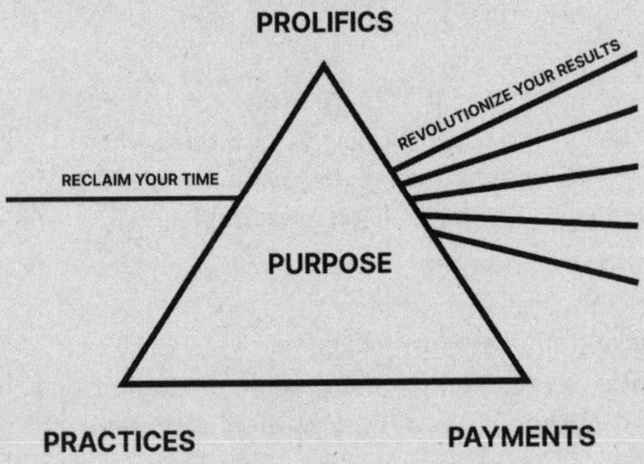

1. Write ten open-ended questions around things you want to do that you feel are challenging. For example, you may want to start a new business, but you don't feel like you have the time, experience, or money to do it.
2. Instead of saying you can't do it because of those barriers, ask what can happen. By leveraging the principles learned in *Time Tipping*, you'll find a creative answer. Like this: How can ABC happen, without XYZ happening, by UNREALISTIC DATE?

    —Remember, you don't have to be the one who does everything. You're the architect of how you spend your time on your projects. When you don't know how to do something, ask who can do it, what can make it happen, where can it be done, and why it needs to be done. This way, you'll find the how for it to be done.

—Many people don't find answers simply because they are scared of what the answer will mean or what it might take to get the job done. Successful people, however, are more scared of not trying (and the regretful consequences of not doing it) than they are of failing. Make your move by making your better questions bigger than the answers you're afraid of.

3. Now that you have ten open-ended "better questions" around your challenges, share them with an accountability partner.
4. Discuss ways you can eliminate, delegate, and outsource your challenges as a way to mitigate risk and get the result without waiting years to accomplish this goal.

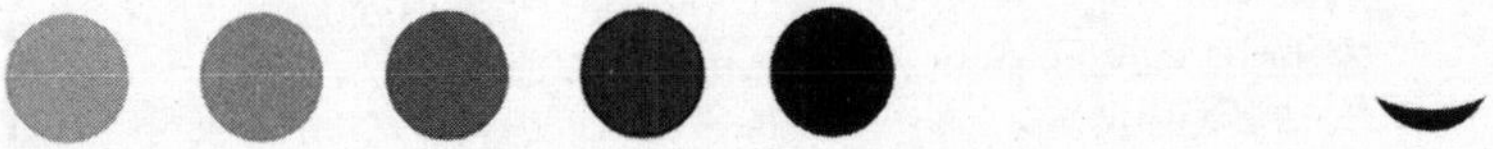

BE PROLIFIC, NOT PERFECT.

EPILOGUE

Be Prolific, Not Perfect

Grif was magic.

Hundreds whooped and cheered that day on that secluded beach. We joined hands in a circle and bore the grief together in a *paddle-out* for my best friend, eight-year-old Grif, who had died the week before. Splashing the water on our surfboards in the middle of the bay, crying in unison—we sang "Aloha 'Oe" and threw lei flowers in mourning with his family.

Life's unfair. Wouldn't it be nice if we didn't have to feel pain? But we do. Wouldn't it be nice if struggles weren't a part of life? But they are. Wouldn't it be nice if we had all the time in the world with those we love? But we don't.

Certainly, Grif had been through more than his fair share of unjust pain and struggles during his short eight years on earth—*but you would never know it by his pure expressions of excitement and joy over every little thing in life.*

His giant and contagious smile, his zest, his complete and total disregard for his own challenges, his unconditional love for every human . . . made Grif the talk of the town.

Grif was the happiest person on earth. Grif, to me, is love.

Ask anyone who knew him, and they'll tell you he loved them and was their best friend too. He was. Grif didn't know how much time he had, but with his short time he became the embodiment of love. Grif inspires me.

Who are you are becoming?

As I tie a bow on this book and look back on the years it took to research, test, and write, I've become aware that prioritizing time is a way to prioritize what you love. Time is about love. Time is an expression of love.

Whether you're spending time, investing time, or sacrificing time—whether it's quality time or quantity time—love shows up by how you spend your time.

May *Time Tipping* help you give and receive what you really want through your work, your art, your relationships, and your life—the gift of love.

Whether you have time for what you love depends more on what you think of yourself than what the world thinks of you.

I hope you choose to pursue a life of meaningful flexibility and autonomy.

Choose to make space for an abundance of happiness—*in the middle of your challenges*—in spite of how little time you have.

Make TIME your mantra: Today Is My Everything.

THIS IS NOT A TEST.
Reply with YES to confirm.

This is your time—*tip it.*

Make today's sunset your reset.

Additional Resources

Bonus! The 90-Day Challenge

Download your *free Time Tipping Toolkit* to move from distraction to action, prioritize attention, and reclaim your life in ninety days. The 90-Day Challenge leads you step-by-step, day-by-day, by project, to help you bring about the lifetime experiences you've been waiting a lifetime to live. The *Time Tipping Toolkit* includes advance access to things I couldn't fit in the book like:

» audio and video life and work lessons

» data, studies, and tools for entrepreneurs and executives

» a brief history on the rise and fall of time management

For ongoing tools, worksheets, and strategies to integrate your *Time Tipping* practice provided by ***Anti-Time Management***, go to: RichieNorton.com/Time.

Let's Connect!

If you enjoyed this book, please share! I'd love to engage with you online.

Speaking, Consulting, or Coaching Inquiries:
Richie@RichieNorton.com

Podcast: RichieNorton.com/Podcast | **Website:** RichieNorton.com | **Instagram**: @richie_norton

Thanks for being cool!

Acknowledgments

Grateful.

I feel completely inadequate and overwhelmed when I think about the number of people, touchpoints, and events that took place to sync this work. I'm so grateful for each transformation, discovery, and perspective-shifting experience that *Time Tippers* agreed to openly share. Thanks to them, now anyone can test their time flexibility and tap into this proven approach.

Without the significant contribution of so many, the integration of these holistic life, business, and time lessons would only be theoretical. Few things can match the sense of joy, happiness, and gratitude I feel to see people reclaim their time and what they do with it.

Joy, happiness, and gratitude are fruits of the same vine. Happiness is in the moment—what's left is gratitude and shared memory.

For the inspiration, courage, and methodical development behind this book, I'm forever humbled and deeply grateful:

—to Natalie, you are everything. There isn't anything I could say here that would come close to expressing the gift of being happily married to you for twenty years! We married young, had children young, and have lived, what seems like, many lives. Your big dreams to go on the road and travel the world for extensive periods of time as a family forced us to work different before it was cool—and make it happen with babies climbing all over the place. They said we couldn't do it. Ha! I look up to you. I respect you. I admire you. I love you.

Thanks for teaching me to love others unconditionally. We've been through hell, but hell won't get through us!

—to my son Raleigh, one of the times when you were risking your life on the spine of a mountain, or in big waves or skydiving, or doing some other obscene feat, I asked you if you were scared. You told me, "That's the point . . . to be brave." When you taught me that the point is being brave, you changed my life. Thanks for teaching me to face fear with purpose.

. . . Oh, and thanks for doing karaoke with me in Osaka, Japan, and in Dongguan, China.

—to my son Cardon, you once told me, "Who said 'great minds think alike'? The opposite is true." So true. Thanks for teaching me the art of channeling creativity. On a muddy back road while we were roadschooling and camping in British Columbia when you were eleven, you turned to me and said you were confused because "Every *million-billion-dollar* company starts with one idea. . . . Lots of people have *billion-million-dollar* ideas, but they don't do it. They wait for somebody else to do it. . . . Why don't you just get out there and do it yourself and you become that billionaire?" From the mouth of babes. Your art, music, and ability to bring ideas to life are thrilling.

—to my son Lincoln, thanks for getting me in the water often to surf where the ideas for this book could fully emerge. The ocean is so healing. When you came out of that coma after being hit by that car, you asked if we were still going shark diving . . . you also told your mom you loved her and asked if she was okay. Good boy. After the accident, instead of approaching life scared and scarred, you approach life like nothing will stop you. That kind of mentality is rare and powerful. You taught me to see hardship from a position of strength and optimism.

—to the happy memory of my son Gavin, who taught me to live.

—to the happy memory of "Unkie" Gavin for exemplifying a passionate life.

—to our awesome foster children, wherever you are now, your strength is beyond anything we've known, and you will always keep us in awe and inspired.

—to my mom and dad for raising me like I was free as a kite while imperceptibly holding the string to keep me grounded.

—to my in-laws for their constant, unconditional love and support.

—to Grif the Great, of course, and his incredible parents, Chris and Taylor Pierce. Natalie and I are inspired by your lives, the way you raise your family, and how you share the gift of Grif with world. Thanks for demonstrating resilience and helping me better understand the principle of mental toughness. Our time across Europe with you was the time of our lives.

—to Ben Hardy, my student turned mentor. Thanks for being the "who" who has helped me refine my ideas, give this book wings, and step into my Future Self. You're a true friend. Thanks also to Lauren and your awesome kids and your generous extended family for being so kind to me in my visits to your home as I worked on this book over the years.

—to my devoted literary agent, Laurie Liss, your leadership and tenacity in keeping me committed to continuously improve my writing were bold, humbling, and meant the world.

—to my Hachette editor, Dan Ambrosio, for taking on this project with such enthusiasm and professionalism, and for believing in me. Thank you and the Hachette team for your suggestions, vision, and high-quality production of this book. Thank you for dealing with the time zones between Hawaii and New York seamlessly. I feel a deep sense of gratitude and relief to be in such good hands.

—to the many *Time Tippers* who agreed to share their stories in the book, including but not limited to Taylor Cummings, John Lee Dumas, Pat Flynn, Gail Halladay, Steve Halladay, Dr. Benjamin Hardy, Neal Hooper, Lamar Innes, Rashell Jarvis, Eevi Jones, Sam Jones, Michelle Jorgensen, Bryce Jurgensmeier, Nellie Jurgensmeier, Maruia Magré, Thiefaine Magré, Cameron Manwaring, John Mashni, Sean McLellan, Angel Naivalu, Jan Oshiro, Greg Pesci, Keira Poulsen, Casy Price, Ramon Ray, Sirah, Shawn Van Dyke, Doug and Lindsey, Laura Wieck, Ben Willson, and Caleb Wojcik.

Also, deep gratitude to the thousands of other *Time Tippers*, including students, clients, friends, family, and those who wanted to remain anonymous.

—to the devotees who took it upon themselves to test the *Time Tipping Framework* and the *Time Tipping Methodology* before they were named as such. I'm also grateful to the wisdom gained from the greats throughout the ages, including Aristotle and the identification of Final Cause. Truly, this book could not have been written without the life examples, insights, failures, and successes of those from the past and the living examples of those in the present. Writing this book was an intentional slow roll, considering the essential application of the methods in a wide variety of interesting situations, locations, and purposes for full effect.

—to Thiefaine Magré and Jase Bennett, my business partners at PROUDUCT, who have been working with me for many years using these principles. It truly is amazing what can be accomplished at work and at home and working from home to create a global, decentralized footprint while having fun (together, individually, and with our families). One of my fondest memories is when we had twenty-four hours before our next meeting, so we flew from Shenzhen to Bangkok for the day. *Time officially tipped.* Epic.

—to Whitney Johnson for teaching me how to disrupt myself and get unstuck, and the power of smart growth. Your kindness, friendship, and ability to create joy while doing the most sophisticated work are incredible. As we've worked together on projects, you've taught me the art of embracing newness with integrity to core principles with a focus on progress. Thank you for helping me be a better me through personal disruption.

—to the memory of Stephen R. Covey, who taught me about leadership. When I asked him how to handle a certain situation with a person, he told me to be their friend without a hidden agenda. This wisdom has served me throughout my life and has been incorporated into the fabric of this book.

—to Stephen M. R. Covey, who taught me self-trust. Thank you for taking the time to teach me, reach out at all the right times, and demonstrate how to extend trust to others by extending trust to me.

You taught me to have confidence in my capacity to learn and deliver results.

—to the experts who helped me in preproduction, including but not limited to Macy Robinson for helping over many years to improve my storytelling and presentation, Kenneth Barnes for editorial wizardry, and Steven Zink for keeping the sources straight. Your early help during the painful first drafts significantly improved the entirety of the process.

—to Sirah for being a light. You taught me what it means to overcome, against all odds.

—to Marshall Goldsmith for showing me the art of "what got you here, won't get you there." You taught me how to widen impact by helping people who care. You've created a network of love among the highest-performing executive coaches in the world. I'm grateful to be a member of the MG100 Coaches.

—to Scott Osman for cultivating leadership and curating community at MG100. You've taught me how to make life richer through friendship, praising others, and highlighting the best of humanity.

—to Ben Willson for using your genius to show others how the implementation of these principles changes lives. Your powerful contributions have giant ripple effects felt far and wide.

—to Drex_jpg for the stunning art. Drex_jpg began making art of my quotes on his own and posting it. When I learned of his work and liked it, I hired him. Over time, I trusted his artistic eye so much that I hired him to do the art for this book—a perfect *Time Tipping* example.

—to Greg Pesci for clarifying the habit of hope and creating comprehensive resources for freelancers worldwide.

—to Mike and Ashley LeMieux for being there with me in Nashville when I thought Hawaii was about to be blown up by a ballistic missile.

—to Uldis Greters for operating an international enterprise without skipping a beat to create freedoms of time for creators that wouldn't be possible otherwise.

—to my podcast guests on *The Richie Norton Show* who help shape thought leadership today, including Gretchen Rubin, Stephen M. R.

Covey, Jeff Goins, Pat Flynn, John Lee Dumas, Susan Cain, Michael Bungay Stanier, Whitney Johnson, Sirah, Chris Ducker, Donald Kelly, Kathy Caprino, Marj Desius, McKenzie Bauer, Ramon Ray, Benjamin Hardy, Marshall Goldsmith, Keith Ferrazzi, Rhett Power, Jacquelyn Umof, Becky Higgins, Paul Cardall, Richard Paul Evans, and many others for sharing their stories. Thank you for fielding my time-freedom questions from the angles of happiness, entrepreneurship, lifestyle, and productivity.

—to my dog Velzy who is always in a good mood. While we walk down the beach, he's heard me do more deals and more coaching calls, and create more projects than anyone else on earth. Good times.

Deep respect,

Richie Norton

Sunset Beach, North Shore of Oahu, Hawaii

January 24, 2022

Notes

Preface

The erroneous cell phone warning about an approaching ballistic missile appeared on cell phones and was reported in "'Wrong Button' Sends Out False Missile Alert," *Honolulu Star Advertiser*, January 13, 2018, www.staradvertiser.com/2018/01/13/breaking-news/emergency-officials-mistakenly-send-out-missile-threat-alert/.

Richie Norton and Natalie Norton. *The Power of Starting Something Stupid: How to Crush Fear, Make Dreams Happen, and Live Without Regret* (Salt Lake City, UT: Shadow Mountain, 2013).

Frederick Taylor's *The Principles of Scientific Management* (New York: Harper & Brothers, 1919) is available, full text, online courtesy of Project Gutenberg at www.gutenberg.org/ebooks/6435.

Introduction

Stephen R. Covey, *The 7 Habits of Highly Effective People: Powerful Lessons in Personal Change* (New York: Simon & Schuster, 1989), 90–91.

Peter Drucker, *Landmarks of Tomorrow* (New York: Harpers, 1959).

See Alcoholics Anonymous, "Is A.A. for You? Twelve Questions Only You Can Answer," www.aa.org/pages/en_us/is-aa-for-you-twelve-questions-only-you-can-answer.

Chapter 1

Whitney Johnson, *Disrupt Yourself* (Cambridge, MA: Harvard Business Review, 2015).

Sirah and I met in Moldova in 2016 where we were both giving TEDx Talks. She's become a close family friend. I interviewed her from Hawaii while she was home in Hollywood and asked her about her life experience and lessons learned. For more details on Sirah and this podcast interview on *The Richie Norton Show*, see "SIRAH—A Light in the Dark," February 23, 2020, https://richienorton.com/2020/02/s1-e23-sirah-a-light-in-the-dark-explicit/.

See Jessica Sager, "Skrillex Nabs Best Dance Recording + Best Dance/Electronica Album Trophies at 2013 Grammys," February 10, 2013, POPCRUSH, https://popcrush.com/skrillex-2013-grammys/.

For more detail on Aristotle and Final Cause, see Andrea Falcon, "Aristotle on Causality," *Stanford Encyclopedia of Philosophy* (2006, revised 2019), https://plato.stanford.edu/entries/aristotle-causality/.

Chapter 2

Dorie Clark, *Stand Out: How to Find Your Breakthrough Idea and Build a Following Around It* (New York: Portfolio/Penguin, 2015).

For information about Benjamin Hardy's writings, see https://benjaminhardy.com.

Chapter 3

Geoffrey James, "45 Quotes from Mr. Rogers That We All Need Today," *Inc.*, August 5, 2019, www.inc.com/geoffrey-james/45-quotes-from-mr-rogers-that-we-all-need-today.html.

Madeleine L'Engle, *A Wrinkle in Time* (New York: Farrar, Straus & Giroux, 1962).

Chairman's letter (Warren Buffett), "To the Shareholders of Berkshire Hathaway, Inc.," 1993, www.berkshirehathaway.com/letters/1993.html.

This is Habit 2 from Stephen R. Covey, *The 7 Habits of Highly Effective People: Powerful Lessons in Personal Change* (New York: Simon & Schuster, 1989).

Formulated by the nineteenth-century Italian-born economist Vilfredo Pareto, the Pareto Principle is commonly referred to as the 80/20 rule in which 20 percent of one's actions results in 80 percent of one's results. For more information, see "Pareto Principle," *APA Dictionary of Psychology*, https://dictionary.apa.org/pareto-principle.

Chapter 4

See Marcus Aurelius, *The Meditations*, bk. 1 (translated by George Long), Internet Classics Archive, http://classics.mit.edu/Antoninus/meditations.mb.txt.

Jim Collins, author of *Good to Great: Why Some Companies Make the Leap and Others Don't* (New York: Harper Business, 2001) and other bestselling works on business leadership and strategy, claims that he learned this maxim of decision-making from legendary management consultant Peter Drucker. Collins mentioned recalling lessons he learned from Peter Drucker in the foreword to the fiftieth anniversary edition of Peter Drucker's *The Effective Executive* (New York: Harper Business, 1967; anniversary ed., 2017).

The Darton Group in its newsletter/blog, *The Darton Equation* (January 2012), made these comments in writing about Walter Isaacson's highly praised biography *Steve Jobs* (New York: Simon & Schuster, 2011), https://dartongroup.wordpress.com/tag/steve-jobs/. Isaacson in his 2011 biography noted the various ways that Jobs used the phrase over the years.

For an overview of Johnson's successful business philosophy, see Jason Feifer, "Dwayne Johnson and Dany Garcia Want You to Rethink Everything," *Entrepreneur* (April 2020; updated March 2021), www.entrepreneur.com/article/348232.

Chapter 5

For background information related to this chapter's epigraph and Aicha Evans's influence on the human spirit and technology, see "Aicha Evans: Human Spirit and Technology," *Disrupt Yourself Podcast with Whitney Johnson* (podcast), May 25, 2021, https://whitneyjohnson.com/wp-content/uploads/2021/05/DisruptYourselfPodcast217AichaEvans.pdf.

For a description of Rodgers's adventure, see Jason Paur, "Sept. 17, 1911: First Transcontinental Flight Takes Weeks," *Wired*, September 17, 2009, www.wired.com/2009/09/0917transcontinental-flight/.

Gerald Smith, "Spanning Time: Before Lindbergh, Another Aviation Pioneer Made Brief Stop in Broome," *Binghamton Press & Sun-Bulletin*, July 19, 2019, www.pressconnects.com/story/news/connections/history/2019/07/20/early-aviation-pioneer-cal-rodgers-made-brief-stop-broome-county/1757428001/.

Ben H. Morrow and K. W. Charles, "Cal Rodgers and the Vin Fiz," *Historic Aviation* (October 1969), www.modelaircraft.org/files/RodgersCalbraithCalPerry.pdf.

Smithsonian National Air and Space Museum, "The First American Transcontinental Flight," https://pioneersofflight.si.edu/content/first-american-transcontinental-flight.

Karen Weise and Daisuke Wakabayashi, "How Andy Jassy, Amazon's Next C.E.O., Was a 'Brain Double' for Jeff Bezos," *New York Times*, February 4, 2021.

See Cal Newport, *Deep Work: Rules for Focused Success in a Distracted World* (New York: Grand Central, 2016).

Chapter 6

Alisa Cohn, *From Start-Up to Grown-Up: Grow Your Leadership to Grow Your Business* (New York: Kogan Page, 2021), 19.

Jeremy Menzies, "The Ghost Ship of Muni Metro (Part 1)," July 21, 2016, www.sfmta.com/blog/ghost-ship-muni-metro-part-1.

Jessica Placzek, "The Buried Ships of San Francisco," www.kqed.org/news/11633087/the-buried-ships-of-san-francisco.

Jessica Placzek, "Why Are Ships Buried Under San Francisco?," www.kqed.org/news/10981586/why-are-there-ships-buried-under-san-francisco.

The Steven Spielberg quote is noted in "Michael Kahn (Film Editor)," June 10, 2018, https://alchetron.com/Michael-Kahn-(film-editor).

For an overview of Johnson's successful business philosophy, see Jason Feifer, "Dwayne Johnson and Dany Garcia Want You to Rethink Everything," *Entrepreneur* (April 2020), www.entrepreneur.com/article/348232.

Caleb Wojcik and Pat Flynn, "The Origin Story Behind SwitchPod," https://switchpod.co/pages/about.

See Dan Sullivan and Benjamin Hardy, *Who Not How: The Formula to Achieve Bigger Goals Through Accelerating Teamwork* (Carlsbad, CA: Hay House, 2000).

Thiefaine Magré, "Do What You Do Best and Outsource the Rest," https://www.linkedin.com/posts/thiefainemagre_productguy-operations-supply chain-activity-6783427167008256000-WQ6U/.

For more information about PROUDUCT, see www.prouduct.com.

Chapter 7

Ralph Waldo Emerson, *The Conduct of Life* (Boston: Houghton, Mifflin, 1859), 86.

See BodyMind Coaching with Laura Wieck, https://thenewbodymind.com/.

For select quotations of Andersen, see "Hans Christian Andersen Quotes," Goodreads, www.goodreads.com/author/quotes/6378.Hans_Christian_Andersen.

Clayton M. Christensen, Efosa Ojomo, and Karen Dillon, *The Prosperity Paradox: How Innovations Can Lift Nations Out of Poverty* (New York: HarperCollins, 2019).

Akhilesh Ganti, "Economic Moat," Investopedia, www.investopedia.com/terms/e/economicmoat.asp.

See the W. Edwards Deming Institute, https://deming.org/quotes/10141/.

Kevin Kelly, "1,000 True Fans," *The Technium* (blog), https://kk.org/thetechnium/1000-true-fans/.

Chapter 8

Adam Grant, "Productivity Isn't About Time Management: It's About Attention Management," *New York Times*, March 28, 2019.

To learn more about Goldsmith's work, see Marshall Goldsmith and Kelly Goldsmith, "How Adults Achieve Happiness," *BusinessWeek*, December 10, 2009, https://marshallgoldsmith.com/articles/how-adults-achieve-happiness/. For more information about Goldsmith's other work, see his website, https://marshallgoldsmith.com/.

Elon Musk, "The Secret Tesla Motors Master Plan (Just Between You and Me)," August 2, 2006, www.tesla.com/blog/secret-tesla-motors-master-plan-just-between-you-and-me.

Marcel Schwantes, "Elon Musk Shows How to Be a Great Leader with What He Calls His 'Single Best Piece of Advice,'" *Inc.*, July 12, 2018, www.inc.com/marcel-schwantes/elon-musk-shows-how-to-be-a-great-leader-with-what-he-calls-his-single-best-piece-of-advice.html.

Chapter 9

Frank Johnson, *The Very Best of Maya Angelou: The Voice of Inspiration* (n.p.: Frank Johnson, 2014).

Kerr Houston, "'Siam Not So Small!' Maps, History, and Gender in *The King and I*," *Camera Obscura* 20, no. 2 (2005): 73–117.

See Ramon Ray, "Entrepreneurship and Depression: Resource for Entrepreneurs to Understand and Conquer It," https://smarthustle.com/entrepreneurship-and-depression/#.YZbql2DMKUk. This website contains additional information about Ramon Ray and his work.

Ivan DeLuce, "Something Profound Happens When Astronauts See Earth from Space for the First Time," *Business Insider*, July 16, 2019, www.businessinsider.com/overview-effect-nasa-apollo8-perspective-awareness-space-2015-8.

Sarah Scoles, "So You Think You Love Earth? Wait Until You See It in VR," *Wired*, June 21, 2016, www.wired.com/2016/06/2047434/.

Chapter 10

These Einstein quotes and their origins were recounted by *Life* magazine editor William Miller from the May 2, 1955, article "Death of a Genius" in *Life* and is available at www.sundheimgroup.com/wp-content/uploads/2018/05/Einstein-article-1955_05.pdf.

Dr. King's quote comes from his sermon of August 11, 1957, delivered in Montgomery, Alabama.

The Steve Jobs quote is from the prepared text of his commencement address delivered at Stanford University, June 12, 2005, https://news.stanford.edu/2005/06/14/jobs-061505/.

Marla Tabaka, "Brené Brown Asked Senior Leaders This Tough Question," *Inc.*, March 28, 2019, www.inc.com/marla-tabaka/brene-brown-asked-senior-leaders-this-tough-question-answer-may-sting-a-bit.html.

Charles Dickens, *A Tale of Two Cities* (Philadelphia: T. B. Peterson and Brothers, 1859), 4–5.

Index